MW00324897

SECRETS OF
THE BLUE BUNGALOW

SECRETS OF THE BLUE BUNGALOW

*More True Tales of Family Life in the
Outer, Outer, Outer, Outer Excelsior*

by

Kevin Fisher-Paulson

TWO PENNY PRESS
SAN FRANCISCO

SECRETS OF THE BLUE BUNGALOW
More True Tales of Family Life in the
Outer, Outer, Outer, Outer Excelsior
by
Kevin Fisher-Paulson

TWO PENNY PRESS
in association with Fearless Literary
www.fearlessbooks.com/Bungalow.htm

ISBN: 978-1-7321850-8-1
LIBRARY OF CONGRESS CONTROL NUMBER:
2023941380

COVER PHOTOGRAPHY, DESIGN & TYPOGRAPHY:
D. Patrick Miller • Fearless Literary Services
www.fearlessbooks.com

ILLUSTRATION:
Joe Phillips
www.joephillips.com

TITLE PAGE PHOTOGRAPH:
Ian Aldridge

Table of Contents

Foreword

I DISCOVERED Kevin Thaddeus Fisher-Paulson about a dozen years ago, while driving to my coffeehouse-office for a morning editing session. I had the radio tuned to San Francisco's National Public Radio affiliate, KQED, and heard Kevin delivering an essay on the subject of the worst day of one's life.

In his case, that was the day he and his husband Brian lost custody of the health-challenged infant triplets they had fostered for a year. This was not because of any malfeasance on their part, but because a conservative, psychologically unstable Christian social worker in Oakland, CA (of all places) had decided that it was better to return the children to their drug-addicted mother than have them continue to be raised by gay dads. When Kevin said on the air that this had been a far worse day than the recent one when he received the umpteenth rejection of his memoir on the same subject, my indie-publisher ears perked up.

To keep this story short, I soon became the publisher of Kevin's memoir *A Song for Lost Angels*: *How Daddy and Papa Fought to Save Their Family.* The Fearless Books edition went on to become a triple finalist in two indie-publishing contests. It also helped him land a weekly column for the San Francisco Chronicle, which he has masterfully written for eight years now. In 2015 I turned the rights to *Song* over to Kevin to publish a second edition under his own imprint, Two Penny Press. In 2019 we cooperatively published a collection of his "greatest hits" from the column up to that point:

How We Keep Spinning… ! the journey of a family in stories.

For the past year I'd felt that it was time for a second collection of Kevin's unforgettable columns, but never got around to bringing it up. When Kevin announced a serious cancer diagnosis in a May 2023 column, I knew the time had arrived. When I emailed him he replied simply, "Great idea!" Hence the book you are reading now.

I never really set out to be a publisher. In my youth I was determined to become a successful novelist, and spent a short time as a crusading investigative reporter before morphing into a magazine feature writer. I was more or less forced into becoming an independent publisher after my first three nonfiction books were placed with three major New York publishers during the 1990s — and every one of them proceeded to handle my work with the greatest disrespect (not to mention questionable ethics) imaginable. Finally, by 1997 I'd had it with the publishing mainstream and decided, somewhat desperately, to launch my own boutique press under the name Fearless Books. At the time I could not see the silver lining about to emerge around the gray, nebulous cloud of my literary career.

While I originally intended only to keep my own writing alive, it wasn't long before I found myself drawn to talented writers who were either already ignored by mainstream publishers, or were likely to be. That eventually led to my Assisted Publishing program producing scores of books outside the mainstream, including Kevin's.

In my unexpectedly varied profession as a publisher, editor, and literary agent, I've assessed countless memoirs and come up with my own Golden Rule for their authors: **It's not about you.** That may sound paradoxical, but what it means is that writing about yourself succeeds only to the degree that readers find themselves in your story. Connecting with readers that way is partly a matter of craft — and Kevin has always displayed a deceptively simple style flowing from an admirable degree of craft — but it owes mostly to one's *intention* as an author. I've seen far too many memoirs that amounted to little more than prolonged kvetching, or a barely disguised attempt to even scores. While Kevin could have easily succumbed to either temptation in the heart-rending story he tells in ***A Song for Lost Angels**,* he didn't. Instead he wrote a captivating saga of devotion, struggle, betrayal, and renewal in a way that connected with readers who truly appreciate "family values," regardless of their sexual orientation or family structures. And he did it all with considerable grace and unexpected humor.

In his beloved column for the Chronicle, Kevin has provided an ongoing, up-to-the-week memoir that has captivated the hearts of many thousands across San Francisco and beyond. His audience skews senior because we're the folks still reading newspapers. But he connects with anyone who's experienced raising a family or being in one — not to mention anyone who loves San Francisco. Or anyone who struggles to hold onto the *kind* part of humankind in the course of daily life. That's why I'm confident, as Kevin's publishing partner, that whether you are a dedicated fan or a newcomer to these stories, you will definitely find yourself amongst them.

— *D. Patrick Miller,* founder
FEARLESS BOOKS & LITERARY SERVICES
May 2023

This Book is Dedicated to:

Crazy Mike, Sasb, the Terry Asten Bennett, Deidre, Sister Lil, the Ottavianos, Brother X, Brother XX, as well as the ghost of Nurse Vivian. Thank you for choosing the Fisher-Paulsons as your family...

and to all those who have lit candles, said prayers, cast spells or in any way sent us pixie dust for the journey

Glossary

OR, You Can't Tell Your Players Without a Scorecard

A READER named Lawrence Rosenfeld wrote: "Dear Kevin (if it's OK to be so informal; I'm sure I'm not the only reader who feels s/he knows you. It's just that you don't know us)."

I had been writing a column for the San Francisco Chronicle for few years, so I already felt like I was on a first name basis with the Bay area, as well as a few readers in Pennsylvania, Ohio, Uruguay, New Zealand... the Outer, Outer, Outer, Outer Excelsior knows no boundaries.

There's a downside: everybody knows the family business. My husband Brian once said, "I wasn't sure what kind of week that I was having, so I waited until the Chronicle came out Wednesday morning."

After 183 Wednesdays in a row, I figured that anything worth knowing about the Fisher-Paulsons was already in print.

But last week Paul Giurlanda wrote and asked whether there was a glossary. What is a *Sasb*? Is a *Zanebug* an animal, mineral or vegetable? How big is a *Kipcap*?

So let's start with:

Nurse Vivian: Everyone called my mother Nurse Vivian, including my father Hap. She was the only registered nurse south of Rockaway Boulevard, and was awarded sainthood the day she sewed Joe McCormick's ear back on.

Bedlam Blue Bungalow: An Arts & Crafts bungalow built in 1926. We painted it the color of the cape Batman wore in the 1960s.

The Fisher-Paulsons make the bedlam for which it is named.

Brother X: Eight years older than I am, the middle Paulson boy found himself wedged between two writers. The oldest brother and I are known to exaggerate (one in a blog, the other in a weekly column for the Voice of the West). The middle brother revolted when we wrote about his accordion playing, and insisted that he be referred to as Brother X. He lives in Xford, Long X and has two children, son of X and daughter of X.

Brother XX: Brother XX was originally called Brother Not X. He never objected to having his name in print, but since X was already taken I called him Not X. He's pointed out to me that if the middle brother is Brother X, and the oldest brother is twice as smart as him, then he should be Brother Double X. Given his preference of beverage, I'm thinking of referring to him as Brother Dos Equis.

Ozone Park: This is the name of a neighborhood in Queens. We grew up on the Irish block. A reader wrote to me that he never believed there was such a thing as South Ozone Park until he had a long layover at Kennedy Airport. I told him that the name of my birth neighborhood was established in 1882, because it meant that good breezes from the ocean ran through there. Starting in 1948, the breezes from the airplanes at Idlewild Airport came in as well.

The Outer, Outer, Outer, Outer Excelsior: There are four outers to the Excelsior, which is exactly how I like my martini. It's on the very edge of the map of San Francisco — so that an eighth of an inch farther, cartographers write, "Here there be dragons!"

Frank: Nickname for San Francisco. It won out over *"the city by the bay"*; *"Baghdad by the Bay,"*; *"the Big Granola"* and *"Frisco."*

Kipcap: Before we even put in our first dent, the Fisher-Paulsons name our cars. According to my husband, I have crashed: *The Queen Mary, The Whitestar, the Batmobile* and *the Griffin*. He insists that this relates to my driving skills, whereas I insist that I have very bad karma. The Kipcap has been in only three accidents, but then it's got less than 20,000 miles. My husband said not to tell anyone that's the name on the license plate, but true story: in one of those three fender benders, I got out of my car, as did the other driver. She looked at her bumper, looked at my bumper and said, "Have a nice day!" When I asked her whether or not she wanted my contact information, she said, "Don't worry. I read the column. Everyone knows where you live."

Crazy Mike: The Greek chorus of this column, real name of Dwight Michael.

Sasb: We are not a high class family, but occasionally we are high-class adjacent. In this case, my husband Brian was on tour in Peru, and on the night before he returned, I had run out of stamina. I took the boys to the McDonalds at Stonestown because it had no back door and they couldn't escape. I stood in line behind this beautiful blonde who looked as exhausted as I did, which meant that she also had fost-adopt children. We shared that sympathy smile, and looked in the dining area, only to see all four of our children hovering around her husband Mordecai, who had an iPad long before anyone in the Outer, Outer, Outer, Outer Excelsior had one. "I'm Stephanie," she said. Stephanie Ann Schrandt Boone: Sasb.

He Who Must Not Be Named: Leah Garchik came to our Saint Patrick's Day Party last year, and told my son Aidan that whenever Adair Lara mentioned her children in print she gave them five bucks. My youngest son has the heart of an accountant and since that remark has pocketed over five hundred and sixty dollars.

Zanebug: The hero of our story. My oldest son was born with a lot of challenges, and in the great literary tradition he has gone on a vision quest over a mountain and across a prairie. This column makes one promise: he will return.

Aquaman and a Shrivel of Critics

IN THE Outer, Outer, Outer, Outer Excelsior there is a Bedlam Blue Bungalow. Its inhabitants have been seen, on any day from Halloween to Pride Day, dressed as Captain America, Hulk, Iron Man, Superman and even Middle-Aged Mutant Ninja Turtles. We are the Fisher-Paulsons. The girl next door dressed up as Wonder Woman just to go trick-or-treating with us. We named our dog Krypto, so it's a sure bet that we see every superhero film to hit the theater.

Things went downhill last year. Here is how I knew: it was the opening weekend of *The Avengers*, and we had tickets for four at the Alamo. The previews rolled, the room grew dark and Zane didn't show up. Now Zane might skip out on Thurgood Marshall High School. He'd probably skip out on Most Holy Redeemer Church. He would definitely skip out on homework. But he would NEVER skip out on a movie with the Black Panther.

Matters got worse until last summer, when Zane went to a school in Texas where he could learn to use his powers for good. I think of it as the Hogwarts for superheroes. But it's hard on all of us. We get to speak to him for only ten minutes, twice a week, sometime on Monday and sometime on Friday, but we never know when.

Last week *Aquaman* came out. Our other son Aidan wanted me to take five of his classmates to see it. No matter how cynical a seventh grader is, he will always be enthusiastic for the Justice League. We drove to the mystical city of Daly, loaded up on popcorn and sour candy. The girl in the group ordered a latte, and Brian convinced the concessionaires to sell him wine. We found seats in the middle.

This is not the theater column. The Chronicle has a fine shiver of art critics (Wake? Shoal? What is the collective noun for critics? Shrivel!) who comment on the cinema, and Peter Hartlaub has already written that "*Aquaman* swims in the shallow end."

If I was writing the critique, I would say the flaw was in Kym Barrett's costume design. If Green Arrow wears green, and Black Canary wears black then why would she put **Aqua**man in orange? Where's the aqua? Wouldn't that shirt make him Tangerine Man? It has been my experience on this planet that only supervillains come in orange.

My husband Brian ignored my outrage about the color, insisting "We didn't plunk down two hundred dollars to see Jason Mamoa's costume. The whole point is for him to take his shirt *off.*"

Okay, you know how superhero films work. We got an arch-villain, Ocean Master. We got the beautiful and clever heroine, Mera, who does not need to be saved from anything other than her own sarcasm. We got an origin story (bitten by a radioactive goldfish). Plot complications ensued, leading to a threat to the surface world as we knew it.

More than two hours into the movie's two hours and 23 minutes, just when Julie Andrews appeared, the darkest menace our hero had faced yet, my phone pulsed. Zane. From Texas. I spilled my kettle corn over Brian as I rushed for the exit door.

"Zane!"

"Dad, one of my peers wants to speak with you."

An unknown person with a drawl said, "Mr. Paulson, we wanted you to know that Zane's been a jerk for a long time, but this week something happened. He decided to take it all seriously. We really think he's turned a corner."

This is not a sports column either, but any Giant fan can tell you that you gotta turn three corners before you head home. Change with my sons is never symmetric. Two steps forward, three steps backward, a few steps to the side. But Zane had turned one corner.

Zane got back on the phone, "I love you, Dad. I'm sorry I missed Christmas. I'm sorry that I'm gonna miss the Talling of the Boys." If you read the column last year, you know that every New Year's morning, we eat our second round of cinnamon rolls, and then the boys stand in front of the bathroom door, and Brian puts a mark to see how tall they have grown. Last year Zane got close, but was still shorter than his old man.

"It's okay, Zane. The kind of growth you're doing can't be measured in a doorway. "

"Thanks Dad, but I still miss you."

"We're coming to visit next month. We'll make Groundhog Day the best holiday of the year."

Got back into the theater, and the credits were rolling. I can only assume that the surface world was saved, and that Aquaman had found the mermaid of his dreams.

Some days endings are not as important as new beginnings.

Emojis & Decepticons

MY HUSBAND Brian has a knack for languages. You can plop him down on 24th Street, Portsmouth Square, the Eiffel Tower or the Gobi Desert, and he'll gesture and nod until the sommelier brings him the best vintage of Sauvignon Blanc found in local vineyards.

On the other hand, I struggled through high school French, then in college switched to Spanish for no better reason than there was a cute guy in my dorm from Texas.

When Tim was dying of AIDS, he got very depressed. I asked him what goal he always wanted, and he said a college diploma. So, I offered to take one course with him for every four courses he took at City College. Worked out well the first semester when we took The History of Homosexuality in Film. But second semester he chose Japanese. As last wishes go, it wasn't bad, but by the time that I'd gotten down the 46 characters of *hiragana* and *katakana*, Tim was no longer speaking on this plane of existence.

The professor said I had a tin ear for language. And to this day, much as I try to *parlez-vous* with the *hombres*, it still sounds like I'm from Ozone Park.

Brian is also fluent in emoji; I am not. To me, it's hieroglyphics without a Rosetta Stone.

He had to explain the difference between emoticons and emojis. An emoticon is an emotion icon, a representation of a facial expression formed by keyboard characters, such as :-) (a smile).

There's an argument to be made that Abraham Lincoln got this whole thing started. For a transcript of a speech in 1862, the typesetter "accidentally" inserted a semi-colon before a parenthesis: "there is no precedent to your being here yourselves (applause and laughter ;)..." and thus the first winky-face emoticon was born.

Didn't get popularized until 1982, with one of the first computer message boards. Scott E. Fahlman suggested that they use :-) when they intended something to be a joke and :-(when they intended to be serious. In other words, a bunch of engineers couldn't figure out whether they were being funny, so they tried telling each other with punctuation. This would never happen with a group of English professors.

An emoji, however, is a small digital image used to express an idea. The first 176 Emojis were created in 1999 by Shigetaki Kurita, who worked for a Japanese mobile company. I thought the word came from emotion, but emoji actually comes from the Japanese glyphs for picture (e) and character (moji) or pictogram.

For the record, the one used most often is the smiling face with tears on either side, which means that everybody is happy and sad at the same time. It's estimated that 6 billion emojis are sent every single day. The good news is that 45 percent of them are happy faces.

Maybe this is because I'm a writer, a devotee of the muse Calliope, and I prefer words over images. Brian may be better at emoji talk because he's a dancer. He and his fellow devotees of Terpsichore shoot each other streams of two hands shaking, champagne glasses, baby angels and fireworks, and they all know this means "rehearsal on Thursday."

For Brian, they are emoticons. For me, they are decepticons.

There's no shorthand for emotion, but even in the Outer, Outer, Outer, Outer Excelsior it's the 21st century, and I should be getting this by now.

My son Aidan, however, cannot read cursive. In fact, he cannot read emotions on faces. He doesn't even get that Buddyboy growling means, "Don't stand between me and that bacon." But he's fully conversant in emojipedia. He hacks into my cell phone when he pleases, mainly to get my passwords, and he has adopted his Papa's finesse, so much so that he no longer looks me in the eye. I tell him to take out the garbage, and a second later a face with a tongue sticking out appears on my phone.

I get that one, but for the most part emojis are too nuanced. All 2,823 of them look alike. I'm still looking for the emoji that stands for "What-the-heck-does-this-mean?"

But just when I think I'm getting it, I send Brian an emoji of an eggplant to ask if he wants me to cook vegetarian and he sends me an embarrassed face. So, here's what I do. When he sends me a smiling face that is crying at the same time, I reply in longhand: "I-love-you-but-don't-know-what-you're-saying emoji." Brian calls this emoji-impaired.

For me, emojis are like exclamation points. Ninety-nine percent of sentences don't need them. But unless I put one into a text stream, Brian doesn't think I care. I can't get away with "Meet you at Dark Horse for dinner." He wants "DARK HORSE!!!!!!" I can never find the emoji for jazz hands when I need it, so just in case I throw in an extra exclamation mark.

The secret to a good relationship is knowing when to be enthusiastic.

;-)

Last Words

LAST WORDS.

I woke my son Aidan up at 7 o'clock and said, "Let's get you to school."

Aidan snarled, "I told you to get me up at six. I wanted time on my iPad." The short drive from the Outer, Outer, Outer, Outer Excelsior contained a litany of my character flaws, ending with, "You're parking here? Can't you even see it's raining?"

I turned off the ignition and asked, "Are those really the last words that you want to say to me this morning?"

First words.

Twelve years ago, Aidan's first word was "Daddy," whereas my son Zane's first word had been "Batman," which was not a bad guess, given the fact that I put on a utility belt and costume in my quest for justice.

My first words: it goes back to dessert. No meal in Ozone Park was complete without dessert, ice cream or Scooter Pies. Even when Nurse Vivian was a few hours into labor with me, Hap insisted on a bowl of strawberry jello before grabbing the car keys.

For the next thirteen months I watched. If Nurse Vivian made an apple pie, Hap (my father) would race my brothers through the mashed potatoes, hurl the dishes into the sink and run back to the dining room, insisting the pie was better with Velveeta cheese. And a cup of tea. So just before he dug his fork in, Hap would say, "Pass the milk, Vivian."

My attempt to repeat these magic words came out as "Mookabea."

It stuck. She was not Mommy or Mother. She was Vivian. To the neighborhood, she was Nurse Vivian. Whenever any boy in Ozone Park skinned a knee or swallowed a quarter, he ran to Nurse Vivian. There would always be a car accident on Lincoln Street on Saturday evenings (because Aqueduct Racetrack was letting out), and before the ambulance arrived, Nurse Vivian isolated and elevated.

After we brothers grew up and moved out, my parents moved to Saint Petersburg (Florida), which Hap referred to as God's Waiting Room.

They saved their arguing for the bridge table. One time, when Nurse Vivian had bid four no-trump without an ace in her hand, Hap stood up and said, "Does anyone want this woman as his partner?"

The woman sitting across from her said, "I wouldn't let any man talk to me that way. I'd get a good lawyer and a great alimony."

Nurse Vivian smiled. "We're Catholic. We don't do divorce. Only murder."

Nurse Vivian was no angel. First off, she was better at cursing than Hap. Second of all, she was her own woman. She taught herself how to drive in an age when "ladies" didn't drive, because she was "G-d d---ed" if she was going to sit and wait for Hap.

And she always got the last word in any argument.

Indeed, Nurse Vivian was no angel. But as Albert Schweitzer wrote, "A man does not have to be an angel to be a saint."

The Monday before Mother's Day in 2002, a doctor called. He told me that she had cancer and I should get there as soon as possible. I jumped a flight, rented a car in the Tampa Airport, drove across that long bridge and got to the hospital at two in the morning. The security guard said, "No visitors." The one and only time I have ever flashed my badge, I walked right past him.

Nurse Vivian was awake. I sat down on the bed, and she told me which letters to burn, and how she had borrowed Aunt Rita's dress for her own wedding and then threw up on it. She did not tell me how make her meringue.

As I was getting up to go, I said, "I love you, Nurse Vivian." She replied, "Bury me in the green dress. You know, the chiffon that I wore at your brother's wedding? The marriage didn't last but I've always wanted to get a second wearing out of it."

She closed her eyes.

Life is seldom poetic. Most of us don't get a Dickens exit line like, "It is a far, far better rest that I go to than I have ever known."

Most of us are more like Oscar Wilde, "Either this wallpaper goes or I do!"

But we've had a few goodbyes this year. The last time Aidan saw Zane in the Bedlam Blue Bungalow, they were arguing about whether to see *The Skyscraper* or *Hotel Transylvania 3*.

So, as Aidan and I got out of the Kipcap and ran through the storm, the only truth I could yell was "You never know which words will be the last words. You might as well be kind.

"Oh, and bury me in the tuxedo I wore to my first wedding with Papa."

All the Bad Words

THIS explains a little about driving.

During my third attempt at fitting the Kipcap between two Chevys, Aidan, who turns 14 in May, began his campaign: "When do I get my learner's permit?"

My husband Brian, rolling up his window, exhaled, "I'm not going to teach you how to drive until you learn how to curse."

"Daddy doesn't curse and look how he drives."

"Remember the broken bumper on the Queen Mary? The smashed-in door on the Griffin? The Escort that got totaled before it even got a name? It's because your father doesn't know how to curse."

He's right. I can no more operate the f-word than I can a stick shift. Not Brian, one foot on the pedal, one hand on the steering wheel, while he questions the lineage of anyone who drives below 85 mph in the fast lane.

Brian is fluent in the profane, but I am a man of few expletives.

How are emojis like curse words? Neither of them does very well in the print medium but they thrive in other environments. If emojis are the exclamation points of the text stream, then the s-word is the auditory equivalent.

Brian cut his teeth in the Palace Theater performing in the original *La Cage aux Folles*, sharing a dressing room with seven divas who knew fifteen different ways to read your beads. Drag Queens are to cursing as Al Gore is to the internet.

You'd think I would have gotten better at cursing for all my twenty years in jail, but for me it's a lot like fish. While in high school, I worked as the prep cook for London Lennie's Seafood Restaurant, gutting the salmon, scaling the red snapper and cleaning the shrimp... got so bad that cats used to follow me home. And what happened? I have not willingly eaten so much as a sushi roll since 1978.

Same thing with county jail. Just the mundane of, "You little *blank-er*. Give me my *blank-ing blank* before I *blank* your *blanking blank*." Where's the poetry in that? The pizzazz?

I've had enough four-letter words (including tuna) to last a lifetime. In my quarter of a century behind a badge I've been compared to a male appendage, a female dog, a roll of sticks and a person who fornicates. The shock and awe are over.

My non-use of the foul is the one virtue I cling to in this adventure called family. Not that I don't think about it. What parent could raise teenagers and not be tempted to bust out a little non-pro-social language? But the problem is that all the words work backwards. If I call him a *son-of-a-blank*, then obviously I am the *blank*.

No, when I crash the Prius one more time, I curse in French or exhort the way they do in comic books: *Great Krypton! Holy Roman Empire! Thufferin' Thuccotash!*

Brian insists that I suffer from a curse-word-deficiency: "Buddy-boy the dog curses better than you do."

Didn't really think it was a problem until I sent in a column quoting Nurse Vivian as saying, "G-d d---." The copy editor wrote back, "Normally we just say goddamn. Dashes aren't necessary for tame swears."

No man wants this for an epitaph: "He was a tame swearer."

So I asked, and yes, indeed, the Chronicle has a stylebook for obscenities: "Do not use them in stories unless they are part of direct quotation...Try to give the reader the sense without using the specific word…There are four words that require dashes." I would tell you those but then I would be George Carlin.

Still in all, in an age that the president of the United States talks about grabbing a woman by a word that I have never used, the Chronicle's style guide remains the last bastion of civility.

Poor Aidan takes after me. One of his learning challenges turns out to be dis-curse-ia. When Zane out-maneuvered him and he took the fall for the seventeen peanut butter and jelly sandwiches shoved down the furnace vent, the best he could come up with was, "Zane — ALL THE BAD WORDS!"

He's got the concept but not the delivery. There's precious little innocence left in the world, and the last corner of it may just be in the Outer, Outer, Outer, Outer Excelsior, in a Bedlam Blue Bungalow where a little boy named Aidan has his own style guide and you don't need to compare people to genitalia.

Or parallel park.

Lunar New Year

Happy Lunar New Year!

It's the Year of the Pig, which, given my profession, should be good luck. But I miss 2018 already because, if I get my zodiac right, it was the end of my Earth Dog cycle. These are five 12-year cycles, and I don't got another sixty years. The *Chronicle* readership of 2178 will surely check.

Buddyboy also missed the Year of the Earth Dog. He hates Lunar New Year as much as the Fourth of July. It's the Fireworks. We wrap him up in his Thunder Vest, but you won't get him to bark "Gung Hay Fat Choy!" He runs under the bed at the sound of the first Catherine Wheel, and Bandit wags his tail and barks, "Dude, you do know that we're Pekingese, right? Show a little dignity."

Cultural holidays were tough to navigate in Ozone Park, but not in the City-That-Knows-How. San Francisco (Frank) celebrates anything and everything. Back in 1992, on the first April 1ST that I ever spent here, I walked down Market Street, and a peloton of naked bicyclists rode by. A passerby shrugged, "Fool's Day Tradition."

It's the only city where you can walk from the Easter Sunrise Service to the Hunky Jesus Contest.

On Saint Patrick's Day everyone is Irish, and on Pride Day, we add an S to it so that everyone is LGBTQ2S, meaning Lesbian/Gay/Bisexual/Transgender/Queer/2 Spirit/And Straight Allies too! It lets all of us blur the line. One of the straightest cops I know recently told me that he was queer not for the sex part, but because we seemed like more fun.

But there's a thin line between joining in and cultural appropriation. We Fisher-Paulsons worry about these things in the Bedlam Blue Bungalow in the Outer, Outer, Outer, Outer Excelsior. Take Kwanzaa. My son Zane is African American, and my son Aidan is of mystery ancestry, so we wanted to celebrate everyone's heritage we knew about.

Figured we'd get a few winces from our African American friends (I'm dreaming of a White Kwanzaa) but it turned out that none of them had ever celebrated the Feast of First Fruits, so in a way, it was like we explored it together.

My friend Amanda was raised by a Pagan father and a Jewish mother, so she's used to navigating these waters. She takes her traditions "a la carte" eating Hamentashen with a side of bacon and decorating her Christmas tree with Stars of David.

When Aidan's biological brother was adopted, his new Jewish father had a Kveller, or naming ceremony, in synagogue. I was nervous that we'd embarrass them but Amanda counseled, "Just bow your head and mumble. Latin's not that far from Hebrew."

I repaid this favor at Zane's baptism, when I told her, "Don't be surprised when they pour water over the baby. But the good news is there's no mohel."

Other than Buddyboy, we love our holidays, especially the ones we invented: the Talling of the Boys or Snacky Dinner Night.

Take Cinnamon Rolls. I don't make them from scratch. I make them from Pillsbury, but we've baked every holiday morning and when Zane called from Texas he said it was the thing he missed most.

Cameron Mitchell wrote stating that she loved the Fisher-Paulson "family traditions you have established that promote stability and bonding. You make me smile."

Tradition's what you do for three years in a row. Nancy Litton wrote that her friends gather on New Year's Eve and try to figure out the Fisher-Paulson Holiday Quiz.

That's what family does. That's what a city does. We do things together three times. When we celebrate together, it's not cultural appropriation. It's cultural communion.

The San Francisco Chinese New Year Festival and Parade is the oldest and largest event of its kind outside of Asia, the parade dating back to 1958 (so it also was the Year of the Earth Dog!)

It is in this city, where the lion dancers lie down with unicorns, where red envelopes mix with Valentine cards that we have truly found the best of all worlds.

My husband Brian doesn't like Roman Candles or crowds any more than Buddyboy, so we hang out on the other edge of the city, in the inner outer Excelsior and we eat noodles and string beans at Win Garden. We may even read our tarot cards after, because like Amanda, we like to pick and choose.

Instead of a lantern, we light a candle in the window, for Zane, so he knows where home, and where tradition, abide.

Congratulations and be prosperous!

Imbolc, Candlemas, and Hedgehog Day

"Well, what if there is no tomorrow? There wasn't one today."
— *Groundhog Day*

O N FEBRUARY 2ND, the Pagans celebrated Imbolc, halfway between the Winter Solstice and the Vernal Equinox. Winter still reigned, but way far on the horizon was the green of Spring, the beginning of hope. The high priestess wore a crown of candles to acknowledge that light was winning in the battle against shadow.

The Christians turned this into Candlemas, a celebration of the Snowdrops, or Candlemas Bells, the first flower of the year. The priests handed out candles and the congregation believed that the longer the candle, the longer the winter would be.

It was the Germans who turned this into Hedgehog Day, on the assumption that rodents were better than clergy at predicting the weather. But when the Germans got to America, specifically Pennsylvania, hedgehogs were in short supply, so they turned the woodchucks into groundhogs, and in 1887 in Gobbler's Knob, an American tradition began.

Thanks to Bill Murray, and the 1993 movie where February 2ND happened over and over again, we get to celebrate Groundhog Day whenever we want.

This is especially true in Texas, where time passes differently. Brian, Aidan and I flew to El Paso then drove through the Chihuahan desert and over the Dolores Mountains. And, lo, it was

Groundhog Day.

There weren't many signs of winter in Texas, other than:

1. Almost every serpent in the Rattlesnake Museum was asleep. And yes, we did go to see a knot of vipers for our vacation. Turns out Aidan speaks Parsel Tongue.

2. The pool at the Limpia Hotel was closed, and the Rio Limpia (the clear river) had been put away until spring.

But still the Lone Star State wanted to know how much longer until Spring started springing and, being short of groundhogs and hedgehogs both, they went to a place named West Pole, to see whether the armadillo named Bee Cave Bob saw his penumbra. The big difference between him and his Pennsylvania counterpart however, is that if Punxsutawnie Phil is wrong he doesn't become road kill.

Time passes differently in Texas. When we arrived, Zane was all at once grown, skinny and tall, with just the faintest ghost of manhood on his upper lip, and a smile I had not seen in years.

He picked up Aidan and carried him piggyback, introducing him to his fellow students, because that's what Fisher-Paulsons do.

Tradition is what binds a family. We didn't get the baking-pies-for-the-neighbors-together-Thanksgiving this year. We didn't get the cinnamon-rolls-on-Christmas-morning. We're not gonna get the Valentine's-Day-Dinner-with-the-kids-at-Bravo's.

But we got Groundhog Day: lots of Candlemas Carols, and the "Wearing of the Gopher Costumes." And the Talling of the Boys. We got his measurements at last and, indeed, at 5'9" he has become taller than his dads.

And we had fun. Zane pointed out the stars and the mysterious Marfa lights. Aidan discovered new mammals, in this case the Javelina, the ugliest brand of pig that I've ever seen, but still a step up from the Rattlesnake Museum.

We sat on a big old porch and put together jigsaw puzzles. We took pictures at the Sleeping Lion Mountain, and Zane genuinely smiled for every shot.

We had breakfast in a bakery in Alpine, hot cups of coffee, orange juice and a warm loaf of cinnamon bread with butter. As we sat around telling Dad jokes, a glass plate on the other side of the room fell to the floor with an enormous crash, and the four of us laughed because, for once, there was a disaster and not one Fisher-Paulson was to blame.

When we needed to pick up more Hot Cheetohs, Zane walked to the store with me, and for the first time ever carried my groceries: "Oh, George, it's a Groundhog Day miracle!" Maybe just a tiny one, but the Fisher-Paulsons have come to believe the axiom of my mother, Nurse Vivian: "Never say No to a miracle."

Zane's not ready to come home yet, but he's a lot more ready than he was six months ago. Just a little bit, we have begun to believe that our boy will come home one day to the Bedlam Blue Bungalow in the Outer, Outer, Outer, Outer Excelsior.

In the meantime, we got Imbolc. We didn't see any shadows, let alone our own, so the long winter isn't over, but far off we can see the Spring.

So, in our hearts, we have groundhogs every day. Or at the very least, armadillos.

Unoaked Chardonnay

THE SAN FRANCISCO CHRONICLE, founded in 1865, has a long tradition of insightful columnists: Brett Harte, Jack London, Armistead Maupin, Jon Carroll, Art Hoppe. But the greatest of all was Herb Caen.

Trivia buffs: What was the original name of Herb Caen's column? "It's News to Me."

Longtime readers remember that Herb Caen did not have his picture at the top. He had his logo, which consisted of the city skyline with the Transamerica Pyramid bending to fit his name. Apparently, it sagged because he had made fun of it so much.

Nowhere in his category am I. The Sackamenna Kid was the first word in the Chronicle (briefly the Examiner) let alone journalism, and I am merely the Ozone Park Kid, the boy from Oz proving that you can take the boy out of Queens, but you can't take the Queen out of the boy. Herb Caen and I are alike only in that we are both "Dyed-in-the-fog" San Franciscans.

When neighbors ask about my column, I tell them to open the Wednesday paper, and flip to the backside. Unlike arguments with my husband, in the Wednesday Chronicle I get the very last word.

But if the Voice of the West continued the tradition of logos, I would nix the Sales Force Tower. Maybe the roof cow. Or better yet, the Millenium tower, as it is already leaning.

Alas instead of a clever cartoon, I have a photo. Lacking the beauty of my page-mate Leah Garchik, this presents a considerable burden.

My husband Brian picked out the purple shirt and scarlet tie for the photo in my byline, but really, it was Nurse Vivian who picked out the face and she agreed with Pop when he said, "Kevin, you got a face for radio…." The only reason my sons are so handsome is that I did not rely on genetics.

Last year, I met a woman outside the Hall of Justice who insisted that I could not possibly be Kevin Fisher-Paulson, because he was so tall. "After all," she said, "he towers right over that column." Maybe I need a disclaimer: "Objects may appear larger…"

The lesbians down the block threw a party a few months ago, and a passerby grabbed my arm and said, "You really need to get that picture retaken. It makes you look like a fat old Irish bartender."

Regular readers are already nodding: Fat. *Check.* Old. *Check.* Irish. *Check.* All true except, going back to my underemployed days, I did attend mixology school, but I was unable to pass the bar.

Last week I wrote the column about Zane having the faintest whisper of hair on his upper lip.

Which brings me to David Cardenas, the self-proclaimed President of the Zane-and-Aidan Fan Club, Mill Valley Chapter. He wrote of the organization's meeting, "Last night we were tossing back a bottle of unoaked Chardonnay when one of my twisted chums saw your column on the table, took a felt tip pen and sketched in a butch mustache on your photo. I've never heard so many 'Oh. Babys!' We took a vote and unanimously agree that you should grow a big bushy one."

First of all, I'm switching to unoaked Chardonnay. Second of all, if you are gonna chair a Zane-and-Aidan Fan Club, it's definitely better with a cocktail in your hand. Third of all, I'm definitely the kind of guy who gets hunkier the more you drink. But you better check the shelf life.

The mustache story: when I first joined the Sheriff's Department, I decided to grow a mustache sort of like Al Pacino in Serpico. Crazy Mike told me it was easy. All you had to do was stop shaving above your mouth.

It became my winter project. I started the day after swearing in (October 3, 1994), but despite all my coaxing, the follicles refused to cooperate. By Christmas the net result was that it looked like I drank too much chocolate milk. But I persevered. I bought wax and a little comb to make it happy.

We got to Valentine's Day. Brian and I took Tim to see Kinsey Sicks at the New Conservatory (This was pre-children, so we had time for dragapella). As Tim opened his door, he looked at my upper lip and smirked, "Robin Williams. *The Birdcage*."

I shaved the next morning. Some people are not meant to grow mustaches.

So, doodle if you will on the top of this page. Draw me with a pot of gold, draw me with a Donald Trump combover, draw me with a pirate hat, but best of all draw me with my husband and two sons and rescue dogs in the Bedlam Blue Bungalow in the Outer, Outer, Outer, Outer Excelsior. It's where I look best.

Little Orphan Aidan

AIDAN attends St. John's, a Catholic elementary school in Glen Park. At 235 students, it's not the smallest in the diocese, but everyone is on a first name basis. Even so it keeps up traditions of the larger schools: there's a nativity pageant every yuletide guaranteed to make the most cynical weep. There's a pizza sports banquet every spring where even the kid who picked daisies on the soccer field gets a medal.

Sister Shirley has a touch of class, so once a year, she throws a Mother/Daughter tea. Now, you would think this was right down my lane: Darjeeling or Earl Grey, petit-fours, bone china, lace doilies. But if there's one thing certain about Zane and Aidan, you don't bring them to High Tea.

By the time that the Father/Daughter dance was announced, the boys, however, were both feeling a little left out.

As regular readers know, Zane currently attends Hogwarts School for Witchcraft and Wizardry, so only Aidan was home to react when the flyer came out for Mother/Son Bowling.

Either you are sympathetic to this column or you are not. That's how writing works. Those on the Pro-Fisher-Paulson side are thinking, "Couldn't they have a Gay Dad/Straight Son Competitive Ice Cream night, where all the gay parents at the school (that would be Brian and me) take their son to Mitchell's to see whether Dad finishes his Irish Coffee Sundae before Aidan finishes his Grasshopper Pie?"

But if you're unsympathetic, consider the plight of little orphan

Aidan. He didn't pick the parents. He didn't pick the parochial school. This was a lot easier at Harvey Milk Civil Rights Academy, where two dads, a mixed-race family and a pack of rescue dogs was a cliché.

St. John's on the other side, has parents like Ms. Mirna, one of those organized mothers who manages a full-time job, a husband, a startup business, two sons, and still manages to be the class mother for the 7th grade. She goes on every field trip, from the art museum to the gold country. Her word is law, among both the students and the parents. Remember how I am emoji-impaired? So I asked Aidan when she sent the following emojis: A bowling pin. A smiley face. Hands linked. Aidan translated, "Bowling Sunday night. You're the mother."

We sat at the dining room table, and Aidan laid it out, "The boys in the class have got you figured for father, 'cause you do the coaching. The girls got you figured for mother, 'cause you bake the cupcakes."

"And Papa?"

"Kinda the same. Tho the ballet part does tip the scale."

Between two and four million children have an LGBTQ 2 parent, so it's not like Aidan's situation is unique. But it's a lot more rarified in a Catholic School. I've cited all the studies and Aidan still doesn't believe that he's got a better shot than average at turning out normal.

There's an upside to having gay parents. In Kindergarten, when Max and Camille were still singing "The Wheels on the Bus," my boys knew all the words to "I Will Survive." But the downside is when it's time for Mother/Son Bowling, someone feels left out, and someone feels like an imposter.

What does a father do? I drove him to Sea Bowl, and let him eat French Fries for dinner. And I took Papa along with me, because, really, he's as big a mother as I am. While I threw gutter balls, he did shots with the more carefree mothers.

Bowling was the worst possible sport for me to have to prove my maternity. Back in Ozone Park, on the one and only sports team that Hap had ever forced me onto, I stumbled home with the trophy of "League's Worst Bowler" with a season average of 29.

Ms. Mirna had organized the event and got only one complaint. A second grade Mom walked up to her and said, "What's he doing here? If we wanted the husbands along, we would have put that on the flyer." Miss Mirna took a sip of her Chardonnay, her perfectly manicured fingers not once having entered a bowling ball that night: "Honey, Kevin may be a lot of things, but he is no woman's husband. I'd go so far to say that he's a lot more nurturing than some of us...."

Sometimes the universe cooperates. Every other mother on the team was over 100. I was at 59, on the very last frame. I did not throw the ball, so much as I shoved it down the alley, and a few seconds later, every damn pin went down. My first strike.

"And furthermore..." Ms. Mirna took another sip, "He's on my team."

Mercredi Mince

NICK HOPPE's got it easy. His column comes out the second day of the week, so he can write about Fat Tuesday, or Mardi Gras, but I get Ash Wednesday, and, trust me, Mercredi Mince (if Tuesday is fat, Wednesday must be skinny) is a lot harder sell.

Cradle Catholic that I am I didn't much like Ash Wednesday as a boy growing up in Ozone Park. What was so great about a feast where Father Fusco stuck his hand in dirt then smeared it over my forehead? And then there was the fasting and the no-meat thing.

Nurse Vivian was a hit-or-miss cook, and her hits generally involved meat. Thus her Macaroni and Cheese was crunchy at all the wrong times, and her Mrs. Paul's fish sticks still frozen.

And on top of that the "giving up" thing. Father Fusco called it abstinence but I called it hell. He and Sister Mary Magdalen knew exactly where to get you.

"Sister," Brother X would say, "I'm giving up strawberries for the Lord."

"You're allergic to strawberries. You're giving up chocolate."

"Sister," Brother XX would say, "I'm giving up basketball, for the Lord."

"What you're giving up is showers longer than seven minutes."

The year she cut off my comic books I threatened to convert.

But when I got older I began to think of "giving up" as giving over. For six weeks. Half a season. Even though I love chocolate, 40 days away from it (minus the Sundays) led me to appreciate it more.

Some things I gave up for Lent and then never took up again. Like skydiving. And heterosexuality.

It's not always fun. I got to admit that my husband Brian is a lot better at giving up things than I am, but the Lent that he gave up smoking I almost gave up marriage.

But then there's this column. I'm not famous, but I've got this lower simmer of San Francisco celebrity going on that occurs only when inconvenient. Like when Aidan and I stop in Bravo's to pick up a pizza and I tell Aidan that Cheetohs are not a vegetable and he yells, "You're not my real father!" While I get ready for a nice, satisfying blow-up, inevitably a kind stranger puts their hand on my shoulder and says, "Aren't you the guy in the purple shirt? Your sons are so cute. Is this the one who stuck his head in a concrete staircase?"

So whatever I write that I'm abstaining from will be cross-checked by the clerk in the Diamond Heights Safeway: "Didn't you give up ice cream?"

Which brings me to zebras. Another coach at the school is the most generous guy I ever met, always donating to the school, always surprising people with gifts like the time he sprang for Warrior tickets for Zane. His family is very different from ours. Their children do homework, for example. We go bowling. They go big game hunting. The daughter, who's the same age as Zane, showed us a photo of the zebra she took down last summer.

Aidan and I had very different questions. Mine was, "Is that a white horse with black stripes or a black horse with white stripes?"

But not Aidan. A few days later, the coach knocked on my door on a Saturday morning, and he's one of the very few people for whom I would open the door before caffeine. Aidan put down the TV remote, which is in itself a miracle, and said, "Coach, you know that safari you went on?"

Coach smiled, "Yes, Aidan. Someday maybe you could come. It's a lot of fun."

Aidan replied, "Not for the zebra."

I turned bright red but Coach laughed and said, "Aidan, that's part of growing up. We don't have to agree with each other, just respect our differences. And I come from a long line of carnivores."

He left soon after, and Aidan asked, "Daddy, what about us? Are we carnivores or herbivores?"

"We're more like whatever's-in-front-of-us-ivores. But I get what you're saying. We're not ready to become vegetarians, but maybe we can ease in a little tofu."

It's no longer fashionable to give up things for Lent, but then I have never been *au courant*. I'm giving up meat. Just for six weeks (minus the Sundays). I could tell you it's for my health, but I gave up visiting doctors once and never went back.

I could tell you I'm doing it for the environment because live-stock production of methane and nitrous oxides does 25 times the climate change damage that carbon dioxide does. The earth's a big planet, but we'll start with changing the Outer, Outer, Outer, Outer Excelsior.

But really, I'm doing it for Aidan.

And the zebra.

Un Mal pour un Bien

THERE's Crazy Mike and there's Crazy Michele. Both work with me in the San Francisco Sheriff's Office. Both tell me that the other one's strange, which makes me wonder what the two of them say about me when I'm not there.

Crazy Michele called the other day and said she had to leave work because she had just lost her wallet, and she had searched all morning and had to go home to cancel her credit cards.

I've lost more wallets than boyfriends. (Brian said that he tried to lose me once, but I'm his bad penny.) So I said, "Just go home. If I need anything, I'll call Crazy Mike."

She called me three minutes later to say, "My wife found it! Behind the couch. Suddenly the day is good. There ought to be a word for that: When you think you've just had bad luck, but then it doesn't happen, so the rest of the day you feel kind of good?"

She's right. "Dodge the bullet" is a little too literal for our profession but there ought to be a phrase.

Like the time I forgot to do the dishes, and it was Friday the 13th, and I figured my husband Brian would be mad when he got home, but then the bungalow caught on fire, and what with the firefighters and the smoke, Brian never even noticed the plates in the sink.

On Friday night, Brian called to say, "There's a flat on the Bridance (his car). I need to take the Kipcap (my car) to work." Now, my luck leads to potholes, and I've run over every loose nail in the Outer, Outer, Outer, Outer Excelsior, so I knew my weekend was ruined:

I fulfill the gay stereotype as I have no automotive skills. Fixing a flat meant a call to Triple A, which meant a wait of several hours, followed by a surly mechanic who would grumble, "You don't know how to put on a donut?" Followed by another few hours sitting in a tire shop leafing through 2012 copies of *Sports Illustrated*, trying not to feel like an inadequate husband.

But 57 minutes after I dialed, the mechanic said, "Your car's ready. The repair's on us, as you're such a good customer." There's a reputation: Most Flat Tires North of Daly City.

But then, the Fisher-Paulsons excel at disaster: triplets go away forever, and Zane goes across the desert, so an hour-long crisis feels like... serendipity.

Horace Walpole coined that word in 1754, and it was a reference to the Three Princes of Serendip, who discovered treasure by accident. It was once voted one of the hardest words in the English language to translate.

The Dalai Lama said, "Remember that sometimes not getting what you want is a wonderful stroke of luck."

Fifteen years ago, the triplets moved out of the Bedlam Blue Bungalow and somewhere in the world, those triplets turned sweet sixteen this week.

We were at an adoption support group the next week, and this woman knitting a baby blanket said, "Those weren't the children meant for you. Your forever family is another destiny." I wanted to snap the knitting needles out of her hand.

But without that loss, then Zane would not have moved in. Nor Aidan. And for a decade and a half, I have felt abundant and blessed. Even when the road is hard, there are four of us who are family. Six if you count Buddyboy and Bandit, and believe me, they count.

The French would say, *"C'est un mal pour un bien."* Crazy Mike would say broken eggs make a great omelet, or in Paris, quiche.

I asked Sister Lil what word she would use and she said, "Well, it's kind of a miracle-adjacent, not like a burning bush, but more like, 'Thank God I don't have to explain that one to the Reverend Mother.'"

Maybe the word is *lagniappe*. From New Orleans. Mark Twain described it as an old Quechua word, meaning unexpected extra, "like a bit of licorice root or a spool of thread." Like when Brian and I go to the Dark Horse on the one night every six weeks that they make pot roast, and the chef surprises us with a duck meatball or a yam frappe and I'm thinking, "What the heck? An amuse-bouche? For free? On Geneva Avenue?"

And the chef smiles, "A little something for the beginning of the journey."

But then I get it. Each of us has more than enough catastrophes along the way. So, each of us needs to take a moment to savor the little unexpected joys.

Take time to smell the lagniappes.

If You Find a California Quail...

IN OZONE PARK, it was a lot easier to see that spring had sprung. Not only did the sycamore trees bud, but also Nurse Vivian stopped feeding Captain Crunch cereal to the sparrows that got stranded in Queens for the winter.

Spring officially began with Aunt Bea's Saint Patrick's Day party, attendance mandatory. Her Irish neighbors called it the An Tostal, the Festival of Spring, and if you didn't show up, your nearest relative was required to provide proof in either a hospital bill or an obituary.

1986: Al Gore had not yet invented the Internet, and Brian and I had not yet invented gay marriage. We had met the autumn before, had moved in together that winter. I had met his mother, but he had not yet met my Irish Catholic mother, Nurse Vivian.

The test came on the day of the wearin' of the green. We took the Long Island Railroad out to Hicksville and a few blocks later, rang her bell. Aunt Bea, 95 years old, resplendent in a Kelly green cocktail dress, opened the door. Collectively, the Toals, the Paulsons and the Horneckers held their breath. She looked Brian up and down, then right in the eye. "What are you drinking?"

"Scotch," he replied, matching her gaze.

"How do you take it?"

"Neat. In a glass."

She left me with Brian's jacket, walked him right past the bar, right past every aunt and uncle, and over to her cupboard. "Get that for me, will you, honey?" He reached up to the top shelf and got her bottle of Chivas Regal. "We might as well see now what you're made of." She poured the three fingers worth for him, and then herself. She looked him in the eye once more, "*Beannachtam na Femle Padraig*" and the two of them downed their drinks.

For the first time, she noticed me that day, and nodded, "He'll do fine. I'll talk to Vivian."

In Northern California, spring is more subtle: the Symphony playing DeBussy, the kimono exhibit at the Asian Art Museum. Flora buds in the Macy*s windows, but alas, the one true sign of spring in San Francisco, the Giants, play offstage in cities like Scottsdale.

And although the cherries eventually do blossom in Japantown, here in the Outer, Outer, Outer, Outer Excelsior, the California lilacs bloom whenever they damn please, which is to say purple and abundant. Signs of rebirth: Uncle Doya replaced the ceanothus that died of thirst last year, and Aidan noted that our charm of honeybees have moved into the new tree, proving that the Bedlam Blue Bungalow serves as a home even to rescue drones.

From an official perspective, winter ends today at 5:58, which, according to Crazy Mike, is the moment when the sun crosses the celestial equator. Day equals night, which is why we use the Latin term *aequs-nox* or equinox.

For the first time in forty years, the vernal equinox coincides with this full moon, known as the worm moon. Not only that, it's a Super Moon, which I thought meant it orbited Krypton, but Crazy Mike said refers to the size, proving that even to straight men, size matters.

Almanac readers know you can balance an egg on its end on this day. Scientists will tell you that from here until the solstice, birds will sing more.

Now this is a thing my son Aidan can get into, since he learns differently. At thirteen he can neither recite the times table nor spell his middle name. But ornithology? He's all over it.

Unlike Capistrano, the swallows do not return to Frank this week. Do you know what the official bird of San Francisco is? The California Quail. Late afternoon, as we strolled along the edge of McLaren Park, my son Aidan told me why this drives him crazy: "Have you ever seen one, Daddy? No." He pointed out crows, ravens, gulls and mourning doves. "Not one quail."

Near the cow parsnip we spied a chickadee, whistling those distinctive three notes just a little more often than he did in February. And then, a red-tailed hawk wheeled directly above us, his white covert feathers gleaming, almost transparent against the cerulean sky, screeching just a little more than he did before the equinox.

Aidan laughed, "If you find a California quail, let me know." And I scratched his curly hair, grateful that the sun set just a little later these days, that light was winning its battle with shadow, and just for this one last spring, my son was more interested in the bees and the birds than the birds and the bees.

Happy An Tostal.

The Maurice Chevalier Effect

ONE AFTERNOON, near my tiny deck in the backyard of the Bedlam Blue Bungalow, the California lilacs bloomed. Friends came over, including Leah Garchik. Leah told my son about the San Francisco Chronicle columnist Adair Lara who "paid her children five bucks every time they were mentioned in the article." As Aidan never read my column, this had not been a problem.

Each Thursday I read my next week's story to Crazy Mike before it goes to press. I do not read it to my husband Brian, nor my sons, Zane and Aidan, nor my dogs, Buddyboy and Bandit.

Maybe I should. But Brian remembers these thirty-something years differently. He remembers them as a dance, a Tango, and I remember them as a fairy tale.

Turns out everyone remembers things differently. Nurse Vivian had three boys: Brother XX, Brother X and me, who the other two call Brother Y Knot. We grew up in a row house in Ozone Park. On that much we agree, but from there the narratives diverge.

Pop's notion was that, "No Irishman ever ruined a good story by sticking to the facts." But each boy exaggerates in a different way. Brother XX writes a blog, and on the other coast, I tell the tales of the Outer, Outer, Outer, Outer Excelsior. Brother X fancies himself the fact checker, but if there's one thing that Brother XX and I agree on is that Brother X was the one who told the boys to swim in a circle until the whirlpool crashed Jeannie McCormick's pool.

What Brother X doesn't get is that memory only makes the

outline of family history. Each of us colors in the book differently.

In our marriage, Brian and I call this the Maurice Chevalier Effect. We're like Maurice Chevalier in the movie *Gigi*. No longer in his prime, he remembers the decades differently than his love Hermione Gingold does.

"We met at nine (we met at eight).
I was on time (no, you were late).
Ah yes, I remember it well…"

Brian and I remember our first date vividly, but we no longer agree on what we had for dinner last Wednesday.

For the record, we met on October 8, 1985, at my cousin Rita's apartment in Jersey City. Brian wore a charcoal angora sweater, belted at the waist with Catwoman boots. I wore a blue wool blazer, khakis and a striped red tie.

We agree that what ruined Rita's lasagna was the cottage cheese, but from there our narratives diverge. I insist that I chose him and he insists that he chose me. He remembers that we got married illegally in 1987 in a bar in Chelsea by a priest who got defrocked for it. I remember that we got married legally in 2008, at the top of the marble staircase in San Francisco's City Hall, Aidan and Zane (Frodo and Bilbo Fisher-Paulson) serving as ring bearers.

We never remember the same mundane. A few Sundays ago, after mass at Most Holy Redeemer, he raised his eyebrows at what he thought was me checking out this guy in a kilt. I shrugged because, the truth is, I have no idea what the guy looked like, but I was checking out his beagle.

Please don't be shocked. I'm absolutely loyal to my husband, but lately my thoughts have been straying from Buddyboy. It started a few weeks ago, when Aidan asked, "What would we be like if we were the kind of family who lived with Siberian Huskies instead of lap dogs?"

"Well, there'd be a lot more fur, but we'd have a better shot at the Iditarod," I said, but it got me wondering: if we had a German Shepherd, would it make me more butch? If we got a bulldog or a poodle, would it improve my French accent?

Truth is, we don't choose dogs. Dogs choose us. And Greyhounds just don't think that we are their speed. Every one of our companions, from Miss Grrrl to Krypto has chosen the Fisher-Paulsons because, I suppose, we are lap people.

The narratives diverge, but the story remains the same: two men choose each other, and run away to Frank, the city by the Bay. Along the way, more than a dozen dogs choose them. Triplets choose them, for a season. Zane and Aidan choose them, for a lifetime. In this chosen family, there's been a lot of loss, but the underlying theme is joy.

"You wore a gown of gold (I was all in blue)
Am I getting old? (Oh, no, not you.
How strong you were, how young and gay...)"

And Aidan? If Mr. Brettschneider made you read this for English, I owe you a ten spot.

What Not to Say

BECAUSE of his class trip, I took Aidan to school today (my husband Brian usually takes him). While at morning assembly, I ran into the cool teacher, Ms. I. When she gave me a hug, I noticed that her coffee thermos was banged up.

"One of those mornings," she explained. "I left it on top of the car, drove downhill, and broke the wipers. So I called my mother and she said, 'This was a teachable moment.' Don't you hate it when people try to make a virtue out of a busted mug?"

I hugged back, which is what I do instead of giving advice.

Let me segue to this lunch at Farm Shop in Larkspur a few weeks back with a very nice woman who worked for a publishing house. She's a fan of the column.

Her being a publisher meant that I wore my red silk Hermes tie, the one that Brian bought me in Paris, with Theo Mille glasses and a blue wool jacket that makes me look reporterly. Brian calls it my Clark Kent drag. But the necktie meant that I couldn't eat the angry crab pasta or the curried carrot soup, which was a shame as it's the kind of high-falutin' place that serves scissors with the pizza.

I did have the baby beets with candied pecans and goat cheese, as none of this was likely to stain and the vegetables made it look like I was health-conscious.

She suggested dessert, and just saying, "lemon-crusted profiteroles," puts me in a good mood. As we were finishing off the decaf, the woman asked, "Have you ever thought of turning this into a book?"

In principle this sounds splendid, but whereas I am capable of being clever for 750 words at a clip, I wasn't sure I had the stamina to charm my way through twelve chapters.

Before I could express my lack of competence she suggested, "So much of what you write is good advice for families with challenges. Or people on a journey. Maybe you could put together a self-help book?"

This is not an advice column. I leave that to the Dearest of Abbys below the fold, who tells you how to ignore your husband and to how to hang the toilet paper.

No, my column is more of a How-Not-To, a cautionary tale. If you need to know why not to stick your head into a concrete staircase, or confuse Bandit with the neighborhood skunk or flush magnets down the toilet, then keep reading.

My particular expertise is What-Not-To-Say.

I get this from Nurse Vivian, a practical woman who had lived through the Depression, the Great Johnstown Flood and a World War. She had a high threshold for tragedy.

She had a couple of stock lines like "Layo for meddlers" and "The apple don't fall far from the tree." But the one I hated was "What's allotted will never be blotted," which she would say as she was stitching up your leg or taking you to see the principal.

Take Crazy Mike. Four years ago, Brother X called me late on a Saturday night to tell me that Pop died. Brian was on tour, so I scrambled to make plane reservations and pack suitcases for the boys when the phone rang. The best Crazy Mike could come up with was, "Now you're nobody's little boy." I had not started crying until that moment.

A malaprop is an incorrect use of a word, generally with something that sounds like it, like Yogi Berra announcing that "Texas has a lot of electric votes." Or Dan Quayle, "Republicans understand the importance of bondage between a mother and a child." I'm talking more like mal-a-nice, as in you're going for kind, but you come off as annoying.

So, if I ever were to give advice, it would be never to say the following:

1. "This is a learning experience." When the dining room's on fire, no one wants to know that it will make them wiser.
2. "What doesn't kill you makes you stronger." This is guaranteed to make me want to kill the person saying this, just to see if they get stronger in the process.
3. "It is what it is." To which I reply, "Unless of course this is a parallel universe."

Brian's least favorite phrase to hear in moments of crisis? "We're out of wine."

If you ever see me lying in the middle of the intersection of 18th and Castro, don't say, "Gosh, I know just how you feel." Instead, go for "So that's what you're writing in next week's column." I'll probably give you a hug.

Lotta's Fountain

THE CITY that Does Indeed Sleep: Charlotte Mignon Crabtree left New York when her family moved to the city I would eventually call Frank in 1856. At the age of nine she began performing. She sang and played the banjo, at the Gaieties, a Temple of Mirth and Song, where she became known as "Miss Lotta, the San Francisco favorite." As she danced on barrels, miners threw gold dust at her feet and her mother, who doubled as agent, collected the nuggets, which she carried around in a large leather bag.

By the 1870's Lotta was the highest paid actress in the United States, which meant that her mother had to upgrade to a steamer trunk, and Lotta toured extensively. But she never forgot San Francisco, and when she returned in 1875, she built a 24-foot-high cast iron fountain, painted bronze and decorated with griffins and lions' heads at the corner of Market, Geary and Kearney.

It is San Francisco's oldest monument.

On Wednesday, April 18, 1906, at 5:12 am, a 7.9 magnitude quake ruptured along almost 300 miles of the San Andreas Fault, from San Juan Bautista to Cape Mendocino. Shocks were felt from Oregon to Nevada. The quake, and the ensuing fire, caused between seven hundred and three thousand deaths, making it one of the most fatal natural disasters in history. The city burned for four days and nights, resulting in the destruction of 25,000 buildings.

The blaze would have taken out all the Mission as well, had it not been for the Greenberg hydrant at Church and 20th. The "little giant" kept pumping after most of the others had failed, and its waters saved the Church of Mission Dolores.

As the ashes cooled, survivors gathered at the one reliable structure, Lotta's Fountain. And have gathered ever since.

Like Lotta Crabtree, my husband Brian and I moved out of New York, "the city that never sleeps" to live in the city that often naps. We came to love the fact that, unlike New York, Frank doesn't stay up til all hours, crazy to prove itself, subways churning, taxis honking. Here at three in the morning, there is only the cool of the mist and the foghorn on the bay.

I worked midnight watch for a while back in the '90's. In fact, that's when I met Crazy Mike. We ate apple pie at midnight, played Christmas carols in July, and once in a while, watched dawn on the roof, exultant that the sun was rising over the most splendid city in creation.

There are challenges to working graveyard shift. We lost all sense of time. Another deputy, let's call him Deputy B, walked up to me one shift at 2:52 am saying, "Can you run me over to Walgreens at 18th and Castro?"

"At three in the morning?"

"Yeah, I forgot today's Christmas. It's the only place open." His brother later told me that everyone in the family got either Alka Seltzer or a Chia pet for a gift.

But other than our jail and one drug store, not much is open all night, and 364 nights, we like that.

A few years ago, my boss invited us to Lotta's Fountain on April 18. She told us that she'd buy breakfast for any of us who showed up. And really, this is San Francisco at its best: the mayor, the fire chief, the sheriff, the police chief. Willie Brown and Leah Garchik. Emperor Norton and Lillian Coit. At 5:12 am, we paused in silence, remembering the dead, and then we sounded every siren we could get our hands on, because we still live. At the end, we sang, *"San Francisco, open your Golden Gate... here is your wandring one saying I'll wander no more."*

We then went over to Dolores Park, where we all helped paint the "little giant" in gold.

Remember how nothing's open all night? Five of us, walking upper Market, looking for a place to get breakfast, finding the only restaurant open was Orphan Andy's. Picture this if you will, five command staff members in full dress uniform, sitting at the counter, eating omelets and making small talk with the club boys and drag queens. Best breakfast ever.

Every year I say I'm not gonna get up for it, and every April, the spirit of the city whispers in my ear, and I hurry downtown.

So if the spirit wakes you up early tomorrow, meet us at Market and Kearney. Can't tell you who will show up, and it might be a challenge to find a place for breakfast afterwards, but it's nice to know that even if this is not the city that never sleeps, once a year it gets up real early.

The Great Fifty Days

ARCHBISHOP MOLLOY (my high school) was located on Queens Boulevard in Queens, which in the movie business would be called foreshadowing. Junior Year, Nestor Danneluck, a fellow mathlete of the Math team (the Fighting π-rish), memorized the New York City Subway map: all 27 lines, all 472 stations, from Aqueduct to Zerega Avenue.

"Nester," I said, over my soft pretzel and diet coke, "I'm not sure you should be telling people. The're gonna think you're dorky."

Nester, chewing his tuna fish, replied, "The pot calling the kettle nerd."

"All right then," I asked, "Why the subway map?"

He shrugged, "It's what I believe in."

Every nerd has a category. *Star Wars. X-Men. Walking Dead.* Took me a while to figure out that I was a Catholic nerd: yes, thurifer in college, I knew the obscure, like what to call the last day of Lent (Tenebrae). So I can tell you that this column comes out during Paschaltide, 50 days between Easter and Pentecost. Our long Lent is over.

Let's recap: it began with Father Matt, at Most Holy Redeemer, reaching his hand into a cup of ashes, to remind us that we are dust and unto dust we shall return. There were three significant events this season:

1. Leah Garchik told my son, Aidan, that he ought to get five dollars per mention in the column. On the upside of this, he

actually reads my column now, but on the downside, he is now aware I write about him, so he tends not to tell me the better gossip of the seventh grade.

2. The Son-Too-Expensive-To-Name learned that hamburgers came from creatures who looked like Roof Cow. So, we gave up meat for Lent. But at the first sight of pasta primavera, he announced that he wanted his vegetarian spaghetti with meatballs.

Before I get to the third event, let me tell you about Holy Week 19 years ago. A roofer re-shingled the top of the Bedlam Blue Bungalow, our home. Brian had a dance concert on Good Friday the 13th, and so the man said, "Go on. All I need to do is solder this last gutter."

True fact: do you know what they used for insulation when they built the Bedlam Blue Bungalow in 1926? Newspapers. (Readers be calm. No Chronicle was harmed in the production of this column.)

Three hours later, just as Brian was taking his fourth curtain call, the phone rang. Jon, a good four years before he became Uncle Jon. "Your house is on fire." As we raced home, Jon, and his then-wife Monica, rushed into the house. Priorities: Jon picked up all three hounds and whisked them into his car. And Monica? Sirens wailing, firefighters with hoses, she took each Waterford crystal drop off the chandelier.

A few months later, Monica and Jon divorced. It might have been that he was gay. It might have been that her boyfriend moved in with them. But I think it was the chandelier. Which brings me to:

3. On the Monday of Holy Week, the eight-hundred-year-old Cathedral of Notre Dame burst into flames. Hundreds of firefighters rushed to the Ile de la Cité, to save the very heart of France.

Father Jean-Marc Fourner ran into the burning church, the main tower collapsing, to save the Crown of Thorns. Brought to Paris by King Louis the IX in the 13th Century, from one perspective, it is the very essence of Christianity, a relic from the man who got the whole religion started. From another perspective it's a hunk of wood.

Pekingese or Waterford crystal or wreath of spiked rushes. We each of us reach into the ashes for that which we find sacred.

Before I get to the end, let me tell you about one more fire: ten years ago, Brian and I woke up to the sound of one of those smoke detectors. We rushed out to the kitchen to find smoke billowing out of the microwave. After we opened the windows, we walked into their bedroom to find Zane and the Son-Too-Expensive-To-Name under their respective covers. Took them an hour to admit that they had thrown a box of pencils into the microwave.

We didn't save those Ticonderogas. Nor that Samsung.

We stuck our hands in the ashes and we saved curiosity.

You can rebuild a bungalow. You can rebuild a rose window. But you cannot rebuild a heart. We made them promise to wait for the Dads before any more science experiments.

What do we celebrate in the Outer, Outer, Outer, Outer Excelsior, on these, the great fifty days? We celebrate Zane and the Son-Too-Expensive-To-Name, the Best Boys in the World, and the adventure they bring us.

Like Nestor Danneluck, it's what we believe in.

Happy Robot Day

NINE MONTHS. July 14th, *le Jour de la Bastille*, was the last day that my son, Zane, had been in the Bedlam Blue Bungalow in the Outer, Outer, Outer, Outer Excelsior. As a family, we've missed Thankgiving, Christmas, Solstice, Easter. We've missed the ordinary days as well, but somehow none of the holidays have felt like holidays.

But last week, the faculty at Zane's school decided to allow him a two-day furlough. He returns in less than a fortnight, so this past Monday's telephone call was pretty joyful. "What do you want to do when you get home, Zane?"

"Just be with you." Anyone who has ever parented a fifteen-year-old will tell you this is better than winning the lottery.

"Anything else?"

"Bravo's Pizza, for sure. I'd like you to make your chili. And your cinnamon rolls." For fourteen years, Zane was never enthusiastic about my culinary skills, but nine months of cafeteria food has made even my cooking taste good. Now truly my chili is an all-day labor of love as I puree all the onions, tomatoes, peppers and carrots the boys would not eat if they could recognize as vegetables, and I smother them in red meat and chilis. The secret to my cinnamon rolls, on the other hand, is that I put no effort into them, other than turning the oven on. The Pillsbury Doughboy does all the work.

"And, Dad? Let's make it a Happy Robot Day."

If you're reading this aloud at the breakfast table, you should do the rest of this column in your best robot voice, perhaps B9 from

Lost in Space or Kitt from *Knight Rider*. The truly retro can go for Robby the Robot in *Forbidden Planet*, though I must warn you: Klaatu Barada Nikto.

Happy Robot Day goes back to when the boys were little, five and seven. One cool foggy Saturday morning, I slept in and woke to giggling in the living room. Buddyboy barked as I got out of bed, and Zane slammed the door shut. "Wait! Don't come in." I tapped my foot impatiently. "One more minute!" Five minutes later, Zane flung the door open, and there in footed pajamas he stood with Aidan, holding up a huge cardboard sign, on which they had drawn fifteen assorted robots. Not Second Generation Robotic Droid Series Two (R2-D2), not Heuristically-programmed ALgorithm (HAL 9000) but Zane's unique brand of ninja mechanoids, breathing fire, shooting lasers and in general keeping the peace.

Zane shouted, "Happy Robot Day!" and Aidan added, "and Robot."

Brian, still in his bathrobe, shrugged and handed me a cup of coffee, so I asked, "Happy Robot Day?"

Zane gave me the exasperated look that only the child of two gay men can muster, and said, "Dad. We're together. We're family. And we're not robots."

Took me til the end of that pot of coffee to get it, the true meaning of the feast: we are all humans stumbling through this world. We make choices, sometimes good, sometimes bad because we are not robots. We choose what we dream. We choose what we love. We choose family.

In a way, it's a misnomer. Happy Robot Day should really be Happy-We're-Not-Robots Day. But the cool thing is that we can celebrate any day. Sometimes twice a month, sometimes not for a couple years. It's useful for holidays that we don't quite fit in with, like a substitute for Mother's Day, or those long Marches when Easter is in April or the drought between Aidan's and Zane's Birthday.

Brian would prefer that we have a robot village to set up under a robot tree, but as it goes, Happy Robot Day is low maintenance. We don't have to wear ugly automaton sweaters or go to church. We don't have to light candles or buy gifts, and its holiday meal consists of the Snacky Dinner.

My son coming home, if only for a weekend, is a festival, a recognition of hope. No longer that little boy in the footed pajamas, he returns and the Fisher-Paulsons gather and we celebrate, something robots could never do.

We toast the best boys in the world, before he goes back, over the mountain, across the desert. And we choose to believe he will come back again.

We'll share it with you, if you want. Any day you want, you can choose family, choose love, choose to celebrate.

Happy Robot Day to you and to all a Good Android.

"Like We're Living Outside Time"

SOUTH BEND, Indiana, refused to go on Daylight Savings Time because it upset the cows, so when I went to college there it was the first time that I lived in a different time zone than my mother, Nurse Vivian.

My freshman year, *Star Wars* came out. There was only one movie theater in South Bend (I'm sure that Mayor Buttigieg has made improvements), and it ran that same movie for eight months. Altogether, I watched the Imperial Death Star get blown up 37 times.

I called Nurse Vivian in Ozone Park and told her about the Force and the Rebellion, and she told me that she and Hap would watch it. The next week, Nurse Vivian opined, "I don't see what you like about it. Seems to me the moral of the story is, 'Turn off the visor and shoot.'"

While the clock remained the same, time passed differently in Eastern Daylight than it did in Eastern Standard Time Zone. The child grew up. The parent grew wise.

This is the week that *The Avengers: Endgame* came out. No reader is surprised at the fact that the Fisher-Paulsons spent two weeks watching all 21 of the prequels, or as Brian called it: "The Bataan Death March of Superhero Movies." Last Friday, I called in sick, and we had a snow day, strawberry pop tarts and coffee fueling our trip from *Captain America* to *Infinity War*.

Comic book nerds are zealots. They have a few rules, including don't bend the pages. Another is that death does not matter. Bucky

Barnes gets killed by the Red Skrull at the end of World War II? Turns out he was in suspended animation. Jor-el and Lara get blown up on the planet Krypton? Turns out they've been in Vegas the past eighty years.

The biggest rule is: **Thou Shalt not Spoil**. Don't tell anyone the ending. Don't tell anyone who dies. Don't tell anyone where Stan Lee appears.

I am a nerd. My husband Brian is a nerd-by-marriage, so he adopted the rules, despite his upbringing. In fact, his mother insisted on starting a book by reading the last chapter. Our boys called her Nana, and Aidan inherited this one trait. He cannot abide a literary secret. His first words were, "The butler did it!"

Episode 7 of *Star Wars*. Despite Nurse Vivian, I still liked the franchise and I waited thirty years. But before I tossed so much as a kernel of popcorn in my mouth Aidan blurted, "I saw this with Uncle Jon last weekend. You're gonna hate it when ----- dies."

Left to his own devices Aidan would tell you that Rosebud was a sled, the Ark of the Covenant was gonna get left in a warehouse and Humphrey Bogart ended up with a French police captain.

For *Endgame*, I was determined to be spoiler-free. The Outer, Outer, Outer, Outer Excelsior went under electronic quarantine: no Facebook, no Twitter, no Instagram.

In the second to last film Doctor Strange used the Eye of Agamotto to look forward in time, and Aidan mused, "That's kind of like what we're doing, Daddy. Like we're living outside time."

This is true for Zane as well. While the clock remains the same, time passes differently in the Central than it does in the Pacific Time Zone.

But the child grows up while the parent grows wise. To me he's still that little boy who left last July, and yet when he returns this coming weekend he might not even fit in his bed.

Peer behind the curtain: this column does not appear by magic. Rather, I wait until the magnets go down the toilet or a head gets stuck in a staircase, and then I start typing, but whatever crisis we have, we have to have it by Thursday night. That's when I call Crazy Mike and say, "Should I tell the story about how the dog got expelled from obedience school?"

If it gets to Friday morning Crazy Mike says, "Tell the muse I'm putting in for overtime."

But every once in a while, I'm in a different time zone than the readers, like the Eye of Agamotto has cast a spell, and who the Fisher-Paulsons are on Thursday afternoon are not the same Fisher-Paulsons the following Wednesday morning when the column sees print.

By this time next week, for example, Zane will have come and gone. The visit will be a victory for him, or not. On this side of the time zone, I can give you no spoilers, other than we will have watched *Endgame*. You readers will know next week, but in the meantime, you get to make up your own ending.

Just be sure to tune in next Wednesday. Same Bat-time. Same Bat-channel.

Same Bat-Bungalow.

Detours Are Part of The Journey

BEFORE you put your car in drive, you've got to look in the rearview mirror.

Parked in front of our row house in South Ozone Park was Hap's (my father's) red Chevrolet station wagon, the kind with fins coming out the back. There was a hole in the floor on the passenger side, which is why Nurse Vivian never wore high heels. Once every few months, Hap drove to Johnstown, Pennsylvania to visit his "outlaws." About four hours in on the drive, we stopped at places like the Bird-in-Hand, for fried tomatoes and apple fritters.

He hated maps, so we never travelled the same way twice, which meant sometimes we got lost. This was usually at night, and Nurse Vivian lost her patience around about the third back country road, farms and trees unlit by anything but the sky, at which point Hap said, "Vivian, I'm following the moon."

One autumn on the Pennsylvania turnpike, the old station wagon gave up her muffler. She wouldn't start, and the three of us shoved it to the side of the road. Then it rained. Nurse Vivian cried, but Hap put his hand on her shoulder. "The flat tires, the traffic cop, Aunt Bea in the rumble seat: they make the journey worth telling, maybe even more than where we're going. What happens on the road is the meaning of the journey."

We sat there and listened to the rain, and we ate the lemon cookies that we had baked. Nurse Vivian said a quick Hail Mary, and got out of the car. She walked out to the highway and stuck out her thumb. The first car stopped. Turns out that the driver of this car was headed for Johnstown. He drove my father to the next gas station, then came back for Nurse Vivian, and while Hap waited for the tow truck, Nurse Vivian got into a stranger's car, and put me in the front seat with her.

Fast forward through the next fifty years: I met a chorus boy named Brian, then in the Broadway production of *La Cage Aux Folles*. We fell in love, got married (illegally) ran away, got married (legally), and for the most part, have lived happily ever after.

We found a bungalow in the Outer, Outer, Outer, Outer Excelsior, which had just enough backyard for our pack of rescue pekes. Sixteen years ago, we fostered newborn triplets, medically fragile. We nursed them to health, and about this time, Brian and I bought an actual car, a blue Saturn Vue we called the Griffin. Buses are all well and good, but just try getting a three-seat stroller onto the BART. We had a year of driving those triplets back and forth across the Bay Bridge to get hernias repaired, and broken bones set, and intestines sewn back together.

Around the ten-thousand mile point, we lost the triplets to the idiocracy that is California's foster care system.

But then Zane, a ten-month-old with challenges, chose us, moved in and once again I became Daddy, and Brian became Papa. Two years later, Aidan, an eight-month-old with other challenges, also chose us.

Somewhen, I crashed the Griffin once too often, and we found a lovely little Prius called Kipcap.

The road has never been straight. We've driven the Kipcap across the bridge when the doctor feared Aidan had meningitis. The Kipcap carried us all the way to Davis for our crippled dog Bandit to have a chance to walk.

We've gotten lost in places like Mendocino County. We've

gotten lost at home. The boys flushed magnets down the toilet and the sewer line broke. Zane got expelled. The dining room burnt down.

Along the way, we told our story to fellow pilgrims, our own Canterbury Tales.

Our longest detour: Zane got lost and went away last summer, over the mountains and across the desert, and the bungalow has not been the same. But this past weekend he had a furlough. I picked him up at the airport and it was the hardest I've ever been hugged.

The weekend was 98% perfect, with lots of Bravo's Pizza, cinnamon rolls and Avengers. On Sunday, I got up early, to start the family supper. Without prompting, Aidan helped Papa sort the beans, and Zane cooked the peppers, and after marinating the pork, and grating the cinnamon, and mincing jalapenos, the boys learned the secret of how I snuck carrots in. A few hours later, the four of us sat down with Uncle Jon and the Terry Asten Bennett. Bandit sat on Terry's foot, poised to pounce if so much as a morsel dropped. Buddyboy sat in the corner, wagging his tail at the fact that all of us, if only for a weekend, were at the same table.

It struck me that this was the way that normal families ate. Just sitting together, holding hands, saying grace, toasting the best boys in the world and eating bowls of thick, red chili. Papa's homemade bread, warm with butter. This was the best rest stop we would ever find.

The next day, I took Zane back to the airport, and the leaving was hard, because now we all remembered why we missed each other. But I kissed him goodbye and said, "For so long you've been going away. It's nice to know you're coming back."

Nurse Vivian was right. Following the moon is all well and good, but sometimes when we're lost we've got to stick out our thumb.

Hap was also right. The rest stop, the detours and even the hitchhiking are all part of the journey.

The Rules of Nicknames

A NICKNAME is a name that is not the person's name assigned at birth. It is not born; it is earned.

A nickname says that we belong to each other so much that we have a *hypocoristic*, which comes from the Greek phrase, "to use child talk with each other." In Viking society, it recognized a bond between two people, so when you started calling your buddy Eric, "the Red" there was a rite, with a gift exchange known as *nafnfestr* (fastening a name).

Sometimes a "nick" can be as simple as a screen name. Thus, Stephanie knows me by my AOL handle Kipcop and I know her as Sasb.

RULE #1 of nicknames is that you don't get to pick. The nickname picks you.

When I worked maximum security at the Hall of Justice, everybody had a moniker: Lady B., Pat-Pat, T-Bone, Naked Ray. A story behind everyone, from cupcakes to frat parties. Crash got his because he totaled a cop car on his first day, and it stuck until he retired.

There was one rookie, who announced on his first day, "From now on, I am Iceman."

No one ever called him Iceman. For one, he was not a mutant with the ability to generate frost. For two, he was not particularly cool. Next week, Sprinkles called him Sack Man. He shrugged his shoulders and accepted the inevitable.

The incarcerated called me "The P-ster" which had less to do with my urination than it did my ability to de-escalate, as in *peace-ter.*

The deputies upgraded that when they gave me a black shirt with a P inside a diamond, and dubbed me Super P or Super for short. I loved the feeling that I belonged, so I let it stick.

Crazy Mike got his AKA because he was a quirky genius, the kind of straight guy who knows all the words to show tunes. I once asked him if he minded the alias and he said, "In a way, it's a compliment, and it's better than my surname." (I used to say, "My friend Mike Gunn," but I said it so fast that it sounded like "my friend my gun" thus I defaulted to his nom de pax.)

But this does bring up:

RULE #2: don't use a nickname to be a jerk. We know the difference between a term of endearment and a term of enfearment, so don't go there. The fourth grade at Saint Anthony of Padua called me Porky, and I carry that with me to this day.

Took me a while to figure out what I didn't like about President Trump, and it's this: he uses nicknames to attack. There's no humor, only malice. In 2016, he lobbed Little Marco and Crooked Hillary. This year it's Sleepy, Creepy Joe, the Nutty Professor, Pocahontas and Alfred E. Neuman. It's a form of harassment, and he does it from a bully pulpit.

There's no defense. If you call him Adolf Twitler or Agent Orange, you have sunk to his level.

They go low, we go high.

For this reason, when I bestow a nickname, my first sobriquet is to go with something neutral like a middle name. Unless it's Aloysius or Hortense it's safe, because it's the name your parents picked as your Plan B, as in "We'll call you Kevin Thaddeus, so if you ever get tired of the Kevin part, you can always use Thad." Works for William Bradley Pitt, Laura Reese Witherspoon, James Paul McCartney and

Robyn Rihanna Fenty.

My husband Brian renamed Zane as Zanebug, because even though our son is already a hand taller than me, he will always be that little boy sitting with me on the rocking chair, reading *Daddy is a Doodlebug.*

Aidan however, has objected to several of his nicknames, including Danny Boy and Ado. His most hated designation? AIDAN TIMOTHY. For some reason he associates that with getting grounded. One day, I borrowed from Armistead Maupin and called him Babycake, and he has been stuck with it ever since.

There used to be a third rule which said, "never use an adverb for a nickname," but then Brian and I started calling each other "Madly," shorthand from the Savage Garden Song to mean that in this family *"I'll love you more with every breath, truly madly deeply do… I want to live like this forever, until the sky falls down on me."*

In a way, Papa and Daddy are nicknames, because they indicate that the boys have a special and unique relationship with us. And as this is the most sacred of christenings, I work each day to be worthy of the title.

In another way, the Bedlam Blue Bungalow and the Outer, Outer, Outer, Outer Excelsior are pseudonyms. They describe a very blue cottage in a mysterious and foggy neighborhood by names that are found on no map and where the sky will never fall.

Madly.

Seven Pumps

LAST SUNDAY, Aidan and I dumped a thousand jigsaw pieces onto the dining room table, our one ambition for a lazy weekend. It was a picture of Batman, and we both went for the early wins. I worked the edges into a frame, and Aidan collected yellows and reds, making the reds into Robin, the greens into the Riddler, and the purple into Catwoman.

That left us with a lot of blue and a lot of grey. Five days have passed, and we still can't eat at the table. We're at that stage where two pieces that don't look like they fit together suddenly do and when we realize those curves make up the Penguin's umbrella. Two bits of green left over from the Riddler are the Joker's hair. When we join them, we tap them loudly onto the table so that the other one knows of the day's little victory.

Late at night, after we've both gone to bed, the utility belt will mysteriously become assembled, by either my husband or Bandit, we never know. We do know that Buddyboy is no help because he eats the pieces he doesn't like.

It's what I like about San Francisco. The pieces don't look like they fit, but the crooked street leads into the Golden Gate, and the T line curves all the way from the donut shop at the edge into the very heart of downtown.

So here goes: last Tuesday, I took the morning off, and we drove up the winding misty Bosworth to get to Starbuck's. Before readers rhapsodize about Philz, Fourbarrel and Peet's, know that we go there for three reasons:

1. The Outer, Outer, Outer, Outer Excelsior is almost perfect in every way, but cafes are not as abundant as California lilacs. In fact, none of the big name cafes will move there.
2. Starbuck's is the shortest distance in the fog between me and caffeine.
3. The Portola baristas are psychic.

Psychic is always better than psycho when it comes to coffee-making. Brian goes in Monday through Friday, and his drink appears before he gets to the front of the line. I go in on weekends, and before I even park, Victor scalds my milk, and as I walk in, he says, "I know you were going to order a grande this morning, but you really need a venti."

Brian and I never go in at the same time, but this particular morning, Luis looked us and said, "Nice to see the couple together."

"How do they know we're together?"

Aidan shrugged. Brian smiled. "Puzzle pieces. We don't look like we match, but you put us next to each other and we fit in a way that no other pieces on the board can."

Married in the eyes of Starbucks.

Further proof the baristas are prescient and that this is the dawning of the Age of Affogato: last week, Victor handed Aidan a cup of oatmeal. I protested, "He always orders a cookie."

Victor smiled and said, "He stuffs those in the cushion of the back seat of your car." Sure enough, I found twelve chocolate-dipped madeleines in varying states of decay, wedged between the backseat and the trunk.

I do not have a sophisticated palate. Give me a three-page wine list and I still respond, "the white one." But now, in any given House of the Green Siren, I order a "Venti Seven Pump Non-Fat Chai Tea

Latte, no water, extra foam."

This buzz of baristas doesn't know I write for the best newspaper in the West, or that I have a badge on under the jacket. They don't know that Brian has danced for presidents. They don't know that the reason Aidan picks up the Chronicle every Wednesday morning is because he's counting the number of times his name appears.

But they remember my order, my particular Venti Seven Pump Non-Fat Chai Tea Latte, no water, extra foam describes me pretty well: sleep-deprived, on a perpetual diet, and more froth than spiced tea.

This is another reason I love San Francisco: the cable cars don't connect to Sutro Tower. Lucca's and Beach Blanket Babylon close for no reason. But on any given street, there's magic: tiled staircases, three-story murals and cappuccino artists who read minds.

These green-aproned mystics tell the story of how I'm married to the Skinny Cinnamon Dolce, no foam, extra sprinkles, raising two hot chocolates, heavy on the whipped cream.

They know I'm gonna sprinkle nutmeg on top before I tip my cup towards my son and toast, "To the best boys in the world." He tips back. The puzzle pieces fit together.

Don't Get Mad at the Fog

CARL SANDBURG got it wrong: the fog doesn't come in on little cat feet, it rolls right over the Southern Hills and into the Outer, Outer, Outer, Outer Excelsior.

Technically, it's called advection fog; when the wind over the Pacific cools the sea mist lower than the dew point. But I don't care about its science. What I love is its mystery (or is that mist-ery?); the curling strands of silver that follow you from the Cow Palace all the way up to the blue LaGrande water tank in McLaren Park.

Yes, I love it most days. Except for last Thursday.

My son Aidan attends Saint John's, a small parochial school tucked away in a petite canyon of Glen Park. In the yard, there are eight rows of aluminum benches. The Kindergarteners sit in the first row, the first graders in the second, all the way up until the eighth graders, who sit on the row that is set off to the side.

During the last week of May, Sister Shirley announces Moving Up Day. The kindergarteners relocate back a bench, causing the domino effect of the 7th graders finally with a row of one's own. Yes, yes, moving up means moving back. It's a symbol that the students did not fail out or get left back, that after a year of work, they made it one row backward. Silly really, but with the Fisher-Paulson history of expulsion, detention, suspension and retention, it's pretty emotional: "Hooray! We didn't flunk out this year!"

So, I took the morning off and Brian and I took Aidan to the Psychic Starbuck's and toasted that this would be his very last Moving

Up Day, that despite all odds, he had survived. Aidan Timothy Fisher-Paulson had conquered the 7th grade and was ready to carpe the diem out of the 8th. After that, they won't even be numbering the grades.

We got to the school an hour early, and Sister Lil opened the door. The vice-principal, she never has more than three minutes without an adolescent asking her how to spell Renaissance or whether or not to say vespers before compline. But that day, Brian, Sister Lil and I had a full twenty minutes to sip our lattes and for us to tell her that eight years of teaching Fisher-Paulsons meant she would spend no time in purgatory.

But remember that canyon thing? Well, that's where all the fog went. Every bench was wet, and the students huddled in the gym. Sister Lil was pragmatic, and declared, "Back in the day, Moving Up meant Moving Up. Didn't matter if it was thunder or hail. A wet seat was a sign of a good character."

But Sister Shirley, the principal, said, "We'll wait for a sunny day. We will do Assembly in the gym."

Now, I love me my Ursuline nuns, and I know better than to disagree with the Abbess, but still I was disappointed. This was the symbol that we made it. It may have taken an extra year or two, but we had gotten our boys through grade school. And this year had a little too much moving away. We needed a Moving Up.

Two lessons at the end of the school year:

1. Don't get mad at the fog. If you must, blame the Bernoulli Effect. The fog has been my friend for decades, no matter whether I call it Carl, Karlotta, or Advection. It's what makes us different from Bayonne or Bakersfield. Not to make disparaging remarks about the weather patterns of other municipalities, but I like it here. We live in a city where a sweater

is always cozy, and no one needs an air conditioner. Our hot spells never last more than three days, and we are always saved by that cavalry of fog riding over the Twin Peaks.

2. If the sun, and Sister Shirley, are not cooperating, make your own Moving Up day. That Batman jigsaw puzzle that we wrote about in last week's column? Brian worked and worked it, connecting piece by piece of gray leotard, marrying 973 tessellates, leaving Aidan and me with just 27 pieces of solid blue. Not a line, not a curve. Just parts of the cape. Roughly all the same shape. We sat there, rotating each and every loop within each and every socket. Got down to 5. These were tighty whiteys. No matter which of the five gaping holes we tried, they refused to fit. An hour past bedtime, Aidan took out a roll of scotch tape, and wedged each of the five into the closest possible hole, stating, "We'll take the win."

He's right. Don't give up on the victory dance, even if you're dancing by yourself.

Celebrate every semester. I did a lot of math with Aidan this year, so if I get my numbers right, I just moved up into the 56th grade.

Pride and Prejudice

UNTIL 1955, San Francisco Deputy Sheriffs and San Francisco Police officers wore a six-pointed silver star, like the kind in those old westerns. But that year, they adopted the seven-pointed star. This stood for the seven virtues. Just in case Sister Mary Florence never taught you catechism: *faith, hope, charity, prudence, temperance, courage* and *justice*.

Now the first irony in this is that at the time, both organizations were lacking in justice. As well as diversity. Take the police. In 1955 there were only 11 black officers, and they were mostly assigned to work "the Southeast Station." They did not allow women to join until 1975. As recently as 1979, in a force of 1640 officers, less than 250 were minority and less than 50 were women. And it wasn't until 1981 that Patrol Officer Woody Tennant became the first openly gay police officer in San Francisco.

For this reason, SF cops did not have a reputation for tolerance.

This may explain why the revolution started here in Frank. Police raids of gay bars, including the Black Cat and the Tay Bush Inn, made the community, then known as homophiles, realize that if they wanted equality, they were gonna need to fight for it. Those officers who wore seven-pointed virtue on their chests while they crammed people into paddy wagons? The irony is they were called the vice squad.

And although New York likes to think it began with Stonewall, the LGBTQ2s got their start here in August 1966, in the Tenderloin,

101 Turk Street, the Compton Cafeteria. Cross-dressing was illegal at the time, and the transgender community found itself the marginalized of the marginalized. The managers of the restaurant called the police to crack down on the trans women who frequented it. When one of the officers attempted to arrest a person for "Female Impersonation," she threw a cup of coffee in his face, dishes got flung, and the rebellion started.

It was New York who first called this the "Pride March" but I wonder whether they should have picked the vice of pride when really the whole movement is about the virtue of courage. It took a lot of courage for a trans woman armed only with a coffee cup to face down a cop with a billy club and a gun.

But to quote the cigarette commercial, we've come a long way baby. The Sheriff's Department and the San Francisco Police are now the most diverse peace officer organizations in the United States.

Ironic also that I wear a star on my chest, as devoted readers will know that I am much better at vice than I am at virtue. It takes a different kind of courage to wear a uniform marching to this year's parade theme: "Generations of Resistance." There are friends who remind me that Dan White was a cop, and not everyone understands that LGBTQ2 officers took up the seven-pointed star because they knew that the way to change the organization was from within. What I lacked in prudence and temperance, I made up for in hope.

We all have different reasons for marching. Brian gets up early on Sunday morning because he lived in a time before he and I could get married, before he and I could raise children in the Outer, Outer, Outer, Outer Excelsior.

And Aidan? Ever the entrepreneur, he marches because he knows that if he makes it to the end, he gets two hours of free iPad time.

There's talk about a Straight Pride March in Boston, and how they wanted Brad Pitt to be their mascot. Clearly these guys have never seen *Troy* or *Interview with a Vampire.*

And this year in Sacramento, the organizers of the Pride march banned uniformed police officers from marching. *Banned.*

But here in San Francisco, you don't need your own separate pride. You don't need to ban anyone. We celebrate together. Gavin Newsom, the guy who first allowed marriage equality? Straight. John, the guy who put the boa and tiara on the roof cow? Straight.

And the peace officers? My boss, Vicki Hennessy. She was hired in 1975, the first Sheriff's class to recruit women, minorities and gays. And last year, the city's first female Sheriff issued a rainbow patch to wear with that star, and Chief Scott of the Police Department followed suit.

Come walk with us and celebrate whatever you choose: vice or virtue. Dive right in. The revolution's just fine.

Be proud and be courageous. Seven points of virtue. And a rainbow of diversity.

Penelope

MR. BRETTSCHNEIDER teaches English at Saint John's Elementary School. He assigned the 7TH grade students (including my son Aidan) to read the *Odyssey* this past year, which meant he also assigned it to the 7TH grade parents (including me).

This was a hard sell. Aidan is a Percy Jackson enthusiast, because he likes his literature in the form of a movie, resolved in two hours. He's not much into long narrative. His version of the Bible? Cut to the crucifixion.

But we persevered, reading about old Odysseus meeting the Cyclops and the Sirens. It goes on about twenty years too long, and by the time we got to the last chapter even I was tired of "rosey-fingered dawn" and Athena popping in and out like *I Dream of Jeannie*. Aidan's synopsis for his book report?

"This guy goes to Troy. Then he comes back."

What stayed with me was Penelope. She's the wife, and while Odysseus was off sunbathing with Calypso, she stayed home, fending off would-be-second husbands. They all think he perished on the trip, and she was a wealthy widow. She told them that she'd be ready to move on, mourn Odysseus and get remarried when she finished her tapestry. All day long, in front of the suitors, she weaved and weaved. They go home, and all night long, she unraveled the stitches.

Family tradition: Hap, my father, sewed a Christmas stocking for every member of the family, out of felt and beads. Nurse Vivian took whatever he sewed, snowmen and angels, and used her nursery magic to put it all together.

This sewing kit was part of Ozone Park Urban Mythology: Joe McCormick insisted Nurse Vivian used it to sew his ear back on.

But Hap and Nurse Vivian were a team: Brother X got a Santa stocking, Brother XX got a drunken reindeer, and mine had sequins and bugle beads. The only one Hap ever refused to sew was for Brother X's first wife and turns out they were divorced before the tree got taken down. The needle speaks true.

We talk about gay marriage, and the Supreme Court, but I knew that we had really made it when Hap handed my husband a Bridance stocking.

Almost blind with macular degeneration, he sewed one for each and every triplet.

So when we adopted Zane and Aidan, I decided that it was my job to sew the stockings, and lacking my father's particular skill, I went with needlepoint. If you've ever done it, you know it takes forever. You sew a hundred stitches and you're lucky if it fills a square inch. But anyone with OCD will tell you that it's the most satisfying of crafts because each and every square gets a stitch. Thread in. Thread out. Thread in. Thread out.

When did I start? About fourteen years ago. Every night after the boys fell asleep (have I mentioned their sleeping disorders?) I got out the embroidery. Forty-two months later, I finished the first. Brian worked the magic that can only be performed by someone who has sewn stage costumes for a living ("Next to a tenor, the wardrobe woman is the touchiest thing in show business") and we turned these cloths into traditions.

By 2017, we had three of the four done, and I even threw pictures of Buddyboy and Bandit into the fourth. But then, that year: Krypto passed away, the kitchen remodel turned into a four-month fiasco, Zane had trouble with school, or lack thereof, and it never got finished.

Last July, Zane went on a journey, over the mountain and across the desert. The Bedlam Blue Bungalow in the Outer, Outer, Outer, Outer Excelsior got a lot quieter. The only good thing about my son being gone was that the stocking got finished. But then came Christmas, and it didn't feel right to hang three on the hearth. And so I started a new tapestry, one of the four Fisher-Paulsons, from a picture we took at the AIDS walk years ago, when the boys were still portable. Foot and a half wide. Maybe ten thousand stitches, I don't know. New Year's. Mardi Gras. Valentine's Day. Easter. A stitch at a time.

This week is Independence Day, next is Bastille. A year since our hero went on his quest. For all these nights, sitting in the rocking chair, a candle burning on the porch, a needle in my hand, it sometimes seemed empty.

Here's the lesson I got from Penelope: all those nights weaving she never lost hope that he would come home.

Zane is the hero of this story, not me. And there are days we cannot help the hero. He's got to sail between Scyllla and Charybdis on his own. And for this he needs courage.

But we who remain, we need patience. We can only stay home and keep the faith, one stitch at a time.

Thread in. Thread out. Thread in. Thread out.

Nurse Vivian (to Everyone)

WHEN WRITING this column, I make mistakes. Most of the time the readers don't know that because the unsung heroes of the San Francisco Chronicle, the copy editors, defend truth against my exaggeration.

"No, not the outer, outer, outer, outer, outer Excelsior," they tell me. "It's the Outer, Outer, Outer, Outer (four) Excelsior. The first outer is La Grande Water Tower, but by the time you get to the fifth you're in San Jose."

Still I get corrections from you readers. And you are usually right when we're talking grammar, but last week someone wrote, "You should try calling Nurse Vivian 'Mother.'"

Nurse Vivian was Nurse Vivian. To everyone. If you were feeling formal, you could call her Mrs. Paulson, but if any of her children tried "Mother" she'd say, "We save that for the convent."

Nurse Vivian was her identity. Vivian was not her legal name, but Grandpa Wise never knew that. The story goes that in Johnstown at the time, baptismal certificates served as birth records. Grandpa Wise didn't want her to be raised Catholic, so Grandma took her child down to Saint Joseph's one night and had her christened on the sly. The parish priest, Father Flanagan, insisted that there was no such saint as Vivian, so Grandma looked up at the stained-glass windows, picked the only female Biblical character she could find and said, "Go with that."

No one ever told Vivian that her legal/liturgical name was Ruth until senior year of Johnstown High School, 1939. The first graduate in her family, she decided that that she didn't want to work at Woolworth's on Franklin Street until she married a coal miner. She applied to Kings County Nursing School in Brooklyn and had no choice but to matriculate as Nurse Candidate Ruth.

That September, the head nurse gave her a day off. And another in October. But then came December and the head nurse scheduled her to work on Christmas day. When she went to ask why, the head nurse said, "Ruth Wise. I have given you off Yom Kippur and Rosh Hashanah. Now you work a shift so the Catholic girls can have a day off."

"Well, then, from now on I'm Nurse Vivian. And no matter what Father Flanagan thinks, it's Catholic."

That's how she introduced herself when she met Hap. That's how she signed her Christmas cards.

Every boy in Ozone Park with a scraped knee knew that you had to go to Nurse Vivian to cure your ills. Every Saturday night when a driver rolled down 131st Street on his way home from Aqueduct Racetrack missed the stop sign and clipped a car, the boys ran to knock on the aluminum door on Sutter Avenue, so that Nurse Vivian would run out with her sewing kit and a tray of ice.

Nurse Vivian only ever prescribed three things:

1. Warm buttered soda bread, the kind with caraway seeds and raisins
2. Blackberry brandy
3. A novena to Saint Jude

She worked swing watch at the Obstetrics Ward of Jamaica Hospital, and much to my dismay it's likely she was on duty the morning that Donald Trump was born.

Brother X chose his name as well. Long before the column, there was *A Song for Lost Angels,* and by the third chapter I had mentioned how poorly he played the accordion, so he said, "From now on, whenever you write about me call me Brother X." It's a thing now. Daughter of X. Son of X. Dog of X.

Which brings me to my son Aidan. Without Zane around, he has room to grow. And growing requires a little rebellion. Last week, we walked to Cordova Market. They have only two kinds of bread, but twenty flavors of ice cream. I handed Aidan a bag with Mint Chocolate Chip, Chocolate, and Caramel Swirl, and he balked.

Aidan's brain is asymmetric. Anger about ice cream is not about ice cream. He vented for three blocks until he got to, "I don't even like the Aidan Timothy. Why did I have to get adopted by someone who'd pick a name like that?"

Arguing at these times does neither of us any good. So I offered, "Your birth mother called you one name, after a man you would never meet. We called you Aidan Timothy to honor Uncle Tim, who died the year you were born. But here's how names work. You don't have to live with either. You pick your own. Go ahead. Nurse Vivian. Brother X. The P-ster. Whatever you want. Just make sure you're true to it."

Aidan shrugged, because teenagers hate getting the wind taken out of their outrage. "Well, at least its not Thaddeus."

Copy editors, please note: turns out that priest was wrong. There indeed was a Saint Vivian. Patron Saint of Hangovers and the Mentally Ill. All in all, right up the Fisher-Paulson tree.

Another Zenith of Our Nadir

THIS COLUMN almost didn't get written.

I pride myself on being the Cal Ripken of Western Journalism, not having missed one deadline for 167 consecutive Wednesdays. What I lack in quality, I make up for in consistency.

This I get from my husband Brian, who hasn't missed a performance in almost four decades as a professional dancer. I've watched him pirouette on a broken foot.

Back in the mid-1980s, however, just a few years into our illegal marriage, he did take a break from Terpsichore. He took a job off Broadway, with Playwrights Horizons, in the costume department.

At this time, the shop was busy working on period piece outfits for such shows as *Sunday in the Park with George, Driving Miss Daisy* and *The Heidi Chronicles*. Imagine if you will that you sewed a bustle that Bernadette Peters could step out of on stage.

This was a high-pressure environment. Brian sewed for two women, and he did a lot of the hand-stitching and pressing. But invariably they would come to opening night, Morgan Freeman's chauffeur cap didn't fit and Ginny would say, "We have reached the zenith of our nadir."

Brian and I came to embrace the term. To us, it meant, this is the absolute worst part of the worst part, but it was also hopeful because, well, things couldn't get any worse.

We've had a lot of zeniths in our almost 35-year relationship:

The night the dining room in the Bedlam Blue Bungalow in the Outer, Outer, Outer, Outer Excelsior went up in flames, we stood in the ashes, mopping water up off the floor, Brian looked at me and nodded, "Yes, the zenith of our nadir."

The afternoon we lost the triplets. The morning that Tim died of AIDS. The day that Zane went away.

Every disaster has an ending. All bleeding eventually stops.

Cataract comes from the Latin word *cataracta* which means "waterfall," which in turn comes from the Greek word katarosso, which means to crash down. Early Persian physicians thought that these obstructions of the eyes were caused by too much humor flowing through the eyes, or as I see it, too many tears.

When the doctor diagnosed me with cataracts, I was all set to make this into Greek tragedy, but not the husband: "They have operations for that. This is like an oil change," he said. "In and out in an hour."

We told Aidan that night, and he asked how serious this was. Brian said, "Oh they've been doing this kind of surgery for decades now." So, I looked it up. First known cataract surgery? 1748, by a French physician named Daviel.

Of course, nothing's routine for the Fisher-Paulsons. Turns out my corneas are also damaged, so even the doctor said, "I have no idea what the outcome will be."

Last Tuesday, I checked in to the eye surgery place on Post Street, and tried to act all calm as I signed off forms that would let a doctor slice my eyeball open with a laser.

A nice nurse named Mary Ann checked me in, and even though she claimed to be Catholic, she had no idea who Saint Lucy was, so I figured I was on my own.

There were eight other people getting cataract surgery at the time, and what with just lying there in a bed, I had nothing to do but listen to their nurses ask if they were ready for the surgery, but here comes the best part. They asked each their height and weight, and it turns out that, yes, I was the heaviest person in the building. When I weighed in at 181, the guy in the bed next to me said, "Wish I could borrow some of yours. They do the anesthesia according to how many pounds you are."

Thanks to my relative immensity, I remember almost nothing of what happened after that. Brian picked me up, my seeing-eye dancer for the week. The left side of my face bandaged up, I went home and slept.

When I awoke, Brian told me all the restrictions the doctor had prescribed: I couldn't shower, I couldn't lift heavy weights, I couldn't drink, I couldn't complain about his driving.

The bandages were too thick for me to put on my glasses. So I couldn't read with my remaining eye. Couldn't watch television. Couldn't type. Couldn't shower. Couldn't shave. Not an ounce of caffeine in my system. Itchy eyeball. But then, I looked at Brian with my one semi-working eye, and he nodded. The zenith of this particular nadir. Life would get better after this.

Until of course, next Tuesday, when we do the other eye.

Cataracts II

CRAZY MIKE's real name is Dwight. Before I send my column to my editor at the San Francisco Chronicle, I read it to Crazy Mike, who can always be counted on to give a blunt opinion. If he asks, "What was the point of that?" I know that I've gotten it wrong and go back to the writing board. About the highest praise I ever get from Mike is, "That will do." But I know the story's really ready when Mike says, "Get rid of all those pesky adverbs, then press send."

But last week he ended with, "You ought to have one in the can, for next week."

"Mike," I protested, "I write for a newspaper, not an oldspaper. I cannot put 'one in the can,' because the crisis we had three weeks ago is never as exciting as the crisis we're going through right now. I'm much more of a seat-of-the-pants kind of writer."

"You're having cataract surgery. What if you can't see?"

"Lovelier thoughts, Michael."

"Huh?"

"A man who knows as many show tunes as you should've seen *Peter Pan* by now. When Peter enters the Darling nursery, he tells them that there are two secrets to flying: pixie dust and lovely thoughts. That is exactly how this family works."

I probably could have used a little of Crazy Mike's pessimism, as this is the first afternoon that I can read the words that I'm typing.

But here it is: "Cataracts II." Sequels rarely manage the charm of the original. There are exceptions of course, *Godfather Part II*, but they are outweighed by *Staying Alive, Phantom Menace, Rocky 38* and, of course, *Godfather Part III*.

But you can't tell the story of the left eye surgery without telling the story of the right. As Chekhov said, if you introduce a gun in the opening scene, you're gonna have to fire it before you close the curtain.

After walking around with stitches in my eyeball for a week, I thought I knew what I was getting into, but the second operation gave me that crazed bloodshot glare such that even the Terry Asten Bennett made me put on sunglasses before she would look at me.

Which leads me to making a spectacle of myself. What they only told me in the fine print was that after surgery I wouldn't be reading any fine print. I'm typing this column in a 24-point font. Bright lights give me a headache in this, the sunniest San Francisco July ever, so I'm wearing sunglasses outside, Foster Grants for the computer, even stronger Foster Grants for reading.

Realization: I make a lousy convalescent. Staying home sounds like fun, but by the end of the first day I couldn't wait to escape the Bedlam Blue Bungalow. This much I've figured out: I don't have enough patience for retirement.

Lovelier thoughts, Kevin #1: I started taking long walks around the Outer, Outer, Outer, Outer Excelsior with my seeing-eye dancer, Brian, and discovered things like the anise biscotti at the Royal Bakery and "The Philosopher's Way," a trail that meanders through McLaren Park. There are fourteen musing stations, and we haven't found them all just yet, but the meandering gave me the time to explain to my son the bocce courts and who Jerry Garcia was and why he got his own amphitheater.

Sometimes the journey is a walk around the park. It gave me the chance to spy things only seen in San Francisco: espresso with a beer chaser.

Uncle Jon took pity on me and whisked Aidan away for an overnight trip to Reno. Sometimes I need an hour away from my teenager to remember that I still like him.

Lovelier Thought, Kevin #2: Between Brian's four jobs and my two, this is the longest amount of time that we have been together in our thirty-five years. And because I have to keep my eyes shut for long periods, his driving doesn't even bother me.

Lovelier Thought, Kevin #3: Blue. Don't ask me to explain the science behind it but before the surgery, blue wasn't nearly as much fun as it is today. It was all basically navy gray to me, but nowadays I got royal, azure, ocean, turquoise, cerulean, and even celestial.

I get to be grateful. I look up and appreciate the distinct Calypso Blue of the LaGrande Water Tank, the Eiffel Tower of the Excelsior, and think, "What a wonderful place I am in. What a wonderful family I have."

Thoughts don't get any lovelier than that.

Dutch Crunch

LET ME THROW an olive branch to San Francisco sourdough lovers: exactly twenty years ago this week, my husband Brian and I moved into the Outer, Outer, Outer, Outer Excelsior, to start the family that would include our sons, Zane and Aidan, and all those rescue dogs. The bungalow wasn't blue then. It was mustard yellow with brown trim, with a century plant in the front yard. The plant blossomed on the day we moved in and hasn't been seen since.

Wild calla lilies inhabited the backyard, growing without any attention whatsoever.

Within a few months, we got involved with the Friends of the Urban Forest. At the time, we had the least canopy foliage of any part of the city, and together with our neighbors we planted Victorian boxwoods, New Zealand tea trees, and, right next to the Bedlam Blue Bungalow, olive trees. This was my father Hap's idea. He told me that during the wars between the Greek city states in ancient times, the winners would, after raping and pillaging, burn down the olive groves. And since an olive tree takes twenty years to mature, to bear fruit, the olive branch became a symbol of lasting peace.

There are three California lilacs with whispery purple buds to remember the triplets. When Tim died, his ashes started a Japanese maple. For Wolfcub, we planted a lime, and for Qp an apple. Buddy-boy urinates lustily on those saplings, unaware that one day he will join the forest.

Two decades means that we have lived under the shade of the

olive branches longer than I lived under the sycamores in South Ozone Park. Zane and Aidan know of only one place to call home.

And for those twenty years we've been as San Francisco as it gets — me working for the San Francisco Sheriff's Department, Brian working for ODC and the San Francisco Ballet, the original Western cliche: the deputy and the dance hall girl.

But we'll never be native San Franciscans. Oh, I've learned to love Gear-ar-deli, though I still find See's easier to pronounce. I can eat more It's-Its than anyone on the block. And Rice-a-Roni, the San Francisco treat, happens to be the one gourmet meal that my husband can cook.

But, try as I might, I'll never like sourdough.

A town is defined by its bread. When I lived in Ozone Park, it was all about the semolina loaves from Stallone's Bakery on Rockaway Boulevard. When I moved to Brooklyn, Amanda taught me the ways to appreciate a good bagel, which largely consisted of serving them with lox, onions and the New York Times (the East Coast Chronicle).

When we moved to California, I just assumed that I would love sourdough. It's been made in San Francisco since the Gold Rush in 1849, when the prospectors and explorers kept the "mother sponge" on their person, so that the leavening would be more active. The scientific name of this wild yeast? *Lactobacillus sanfranciscensis.*

Two cardinal rules in this city:

1. Don't call it Frisco.

2. Eat the sourdough.

I felt disloyal. I proudly consumed Irish coffee, martinis, fortune cookies, but I lived with this secret shame.

Trust the deputies to solve my problem: When you work in a jail all day, lunch becomes very important. There's this one guy we call W, and every Saturday W organized the order for Mr. Pickle or Roxie's or Lunardi's asking everyone on the watch, from the captain to the cadet, what meat and what bread for each sandwich they wanted. The first time he asked me I truly felt like I was one of the boys. When I shamefacedly admitted that I get no kick out of sourdough, he smiled, "It's OK. I'll get you Dutch crunch."

Dutch crunch was a revelation. As the name suggests, it was invented in the Netherlands. There it is called *tijgerbrood*, or tiger bread. What distinguishes it is that it has this golden crispy topping created by painting the top of the dough with a patina of rice flour, yeast, sugar, salt, and butter. In other words, all my favorite food groups. But it bypassed the East Coast as well as the Midwest, and I have found it in San Francisco.

For years, W added in my "Vegetarian on Dutch crunch" (tomato, avocado, sprouts and olives) and we ate in the cafeteria telling stories. It didn't matter whether the bread was whole wheat, sourdough, rye, or Wonder. It mattered only that we broke the bread together.

Not one single olive has ever appeared on the trees next to our home, so it's safe to say that the trees, like the Fisher-Paulsons, have still not matured. But for both of us, our roots are deep in San Francisco.

Big Sky

IN THE Rattlesnake Mountains of Montana, there's a canyon called the Hell's Gate. You ask the locals and you'll get a dozen different stories. The guy who gave us a lift to the car rental told us that, at a bend of the Clark Fork River, that's where the Blackfoot and the Sioux fought the Salish, also called the Flatheads. The Salish must have won because they named the town *Nmesuletkw*, place of frozen water. The French trappers who settled in after mis-pronounced that as Missoula, and the college students who came a century later further mispronounced it as Zoo Town.

Montana is the fourth largest state in the union in terms of land mass, but its population (~1,000,000) is only just a little bigger than that of San Francisco (~884,363). It is a land of ranches, gold mines and the ghost town hall of fame.

It is estimated that 0.43% percent of the statewide population is black, or about 4,094, until last month, when my son Zane moved in, pushing the total to 4,095. Yes, his Texas days are behind him, and even though it's still a thousand miles away, it feels like progress.

Up until last month, of the entirety of the Fisher-Paulson family only one of us had ever spent so much as forty-five minutes in Big Sky Country. This was me. In 1999, on my mission to visit all fifty states before I turned fifty, I hit the southern edge on my way from Idaho to Wyoming. I had coffee there, so it counted.

But my husband Brian, my son Aidan and I all wanted to make sure that Zane was all right, so we went to visit him.

Driving from the airport to Zane's school, we had an "Only-in-

Missoula" moment: Right after a sign for Butte, there was a billboard that read, "The Rocky Creek Lodge Testicle Festival" (Testyfest for short). I figured they served nuts, but really, it's all about eating Rocky Mountain Prairie Oysters, or beef testicles, breaded and deep fried. Aidan's comment? "Is that where we get meatballs from?"

Brian's comment? "I wonder if there's a Miss Testicle? Or an all-you-can-eat testicles contest?"

We looked it up on-line only to discover that the Feast of Cowboy Caviar had been canceled. I wondered for a moment if there was a testosterone drought, but maybe more enlightened minds had given up the shark fin soup of the plains.

A mile further down the road we lost cell phone reception (which I secretly liked), as we drove past the slate blue hills, under that big broad blue firmament, sprinkled lightly with cirrus clouds. After the exit we turned onto a dirt road, which wound past deer and horses and cattle. Brian asked, "Is it me, or do the bulls look nervous? I thought Testyfest was canceled."

We parked, and walked across the creek, and there was Zane, impossibly tall, with that smile that people say he gets from me. There's nothing better than hugging a son you haven't seen in three months.

He introduced us to his cohort. A few said that they waited each week for Zane's letter that had the column in it. One young man, let's call him "L," said, "You wrote a few weeks ago that Zane was on a quest, that he needed to be the hero of his own journey, and I realized that was true for every one of us in this group."

It was a quiet weekend. We spent most of the time on campus, but on Sunday morning, the four of us walked around Beavertail Pond. Montana is also called the Treasure State, because it is rich in sapphire, agates, copper, topaz and silver, but Zane and Aidan knew nothing of this. They only knew the rocks they discovered were flat and perfectly suited to skip across the tarn. For the record, Aidan won with five bounces.

I handed Aidan a pyrite to serve as trophy, and we both knew it was fool's gold, but still he packed it in his suitcase, to remember those few minutes together on a lake.

Time with either of my sons is never enough. We left on Monday, but on those long nights that I miss him, I take comfort that he is, in a Ponderosa Pine Forest in the Sapphire Mountains, sitting in a circle with eight other young men who are each on their own quest. But they are also a fellowship, standing together at the Hell's Gate, working their way towards Heaven. I picture them laughing as Zane opens an envelope and they read the latest pilgrimage of the family in the Bedlam Blue Bungalow in the Outer, Outer, Outer, Outer Excelsior.

It's then I think, maybe I should have skipped the part about the Testicle Festival.

The Battle of Disneyland

I N 1964, not far from Ozone Park, New York hosted the World's Fair. Nurse Vivian and I rode the Q-10 bus to it, and all of the wonders there. We most loved the ride that Joan Crawford had commissioned Walt Disney to build for Pepsi, with more than 300 animatronic robots dressed in costumes from all seven continents, each of them singing the Sherman Brothers' song, "It's a Small World."

Back then it was a technological wonder, truly the magic of the kingdom.

Fear and Loathing in Disneyland: If you read the column three years ago, you know that our last Disneyland trip was a disaster. The Fisher-Paulsons are not well suited to vacation, but on that particular trip all four of us manifested our dysfunction (Zane even made Snow White cry) and after a pitched argument about the Twilight Zone Tower of Terror, my husband Brian declared, "This is the saddest place on Earth. We are never coming here again."

In the Darwinian struggle of parents versus children there is no confrontation more deadly than the Battle of Disneyland.

Anaheim is smarter than Las Vegas. At least what happens in Vegas stays in Vegas, and we know that the house mostly wins, but occasionally loses. But the Mouse always wins. They take the money in advance, with each one of us betting "This will be the magic moment."

For most of us, it means driving seven hours in a car to wait seventy minutes in line, to get dropped or spun around for seven seconds of terror or excitement. It's a metaphor for parenting.

The mystery is hard to come by. I keep going back because twelve years ago, when Zane and Aidan were tots, we sat on the sidewalk watching a parade go by, and Zane's eyebrows went up and he grabbed my arm, dancing, "Daddy, it's the real Buzz Lightyear!"

More often, however, there's the argument about whether to go on Splash Mountain or the Incredi-Coaster, and those resentments last for a lifetime. Me, I pick It's a Small World and both boys roll their eyes. The Awe of 1964 is lost on them.

That night, we stood in the dark for 45 minutes and only later found out that the laser show got canceled. The next night we stood in the dark for 45 minutes and only later found out that the fireworks got cancelled. The mouse had beaten us.

A deputy friend told me that eight years ago, his son asked for a $25 light-up Mickey Mouse Balloon, and no amount of reasoning with him that he couldn't take it on the ride would dissuade him. Last week that same son, who had just turned eighteen, drove five hundred miles down to Southern California and bought the balloon his father had refused. Now *that* is holding a grudge. The mouse had won.

But on to this trip: after three years of therapy we decided to go back. This summer, we invited a normal teenager to go with us, one of the boys in Aidan's class. First of all, we've never spent a lot of time with normal families, so it was something of a surprise to me to find that other teenagers also refused to eat vegetables or brush their teeth. On the plus side, this wasn't our kid, so even if we let him eat M&Ms for breakfast we weren't going to get the dental bill.

Our only agenda was to have no agenda. We checked in to the hotel, and asked the boys which park they wanted to go to? "The pool." And six hours later they were still swimming. The next morning, we took them into the park, and after piloting the Millennium Falcon,

Aidan asked, "Can we go back to the pool?"

Five hundred miles, and the fastest ride he wanted was the hot tub.

We won. No expectations = no disappointment.

Is there magic in the Magic Kingdom? The answer is yes, but only if you put it in there. Let me quote Albert Einstein who said, "There are only two ways to live your life. One is as though nothing is a miracle. The other is as though everything is a miracle."

The last day, Aidan and Joshua spent a full fifteen hours in the pool. I asked, "Don't you think we should go on at least one ride?" So, we took one last stroll into the park, and Aidan, part boy/part man, took my hand and said, "I know where to go. Close your eyes, Dad." And we walked until I heard "... *it's so much that we share that it's time we're aware....*"

And I realized that, indeed, it is a small world after all.

The Nice Ones

EVERY marriage has a nice person and a person who gets things done. Crazy Mike's the nice one. Uncle Jon was the nice one right up until the day Monica divorced him.

In our thirty-five years, Brian's been the nice one. He brings stuffed peppers to the elderly neighbor next door. He writes checks to Saint Jude, Macular Degeneration and the Fresh Meat Festival. I won't let him go near bake sales anymore because he buys them out of brownies, and I end up five pounds heavier.

But you put him in the Kipcap, and Dancer Jekyll becomes Race Car Driver Hyde. At any given moment I may hear:

"First day driving a car?"

"The light doesn't get any greener than that!"

"It says 'Stop' not 'Park'!"

"Put an Uber sticker in your window and forget everything you ever knew about driving."

These declarations are enhanced by non-pro-social terms associating the driver with canine heritage or anatomical parts. Most of the curse words that my two sons, Zane and Aidan, know have been learned from the backseat.

Me, I'm a lousy driver. I can go Code 3 in a cop car but turn off the lights and sirens and I get distracted. Can't tell you how many bumpers I've lost on the way to Safeway. So, when Brian rides shotgun, I get "Is your blinker broken?" and the ever useful "You do know that the gas pedal is the one on the right?"

This is why I let him take the wheel. He's gonna complain about someone's driving. It might as well not be mine. Thus the only time in our marriage when I'm the nice one is when I'm in the passenger seat.

When there aren't enough drivers, he focuses on pedestrians: "Does he really need to read that text in the intersection?"

Took me time to realize that he's talking to the windshield, not the driver. If indeed there was any possibility of him being heard, Brian would just put on a stiff smile and nod. But with just me and the boys as witnesses, he's the Don Rickles of Prius drivers.

Did I mention that Aidan's fourteen now? He asked me when he could get his learner's permit, and I said, "When you can swear as eloquently as your Papa."

Nature versus nurture, it's all hard to tell when you're talking foster care and adoption. And when it's a two-Dad family, there can be competition about who's the role model. Brian would claim that he taught the boys everything they know about sarcasm, and I take credit for them knowing all the words to "I Will Survive" before they entered kindergarten. But this much Aidan definitely gets from me: he's lousy at coarse language. He gets kind of boxed up in his mouth, so when he's really angry, he blurts out things like, "And all the bad words!"

I'll let Papa teach him Profanity 101. This summer I've been doing a chapter of pre-algebra with Aidan every night, but I'm also working on the other rules, like there are three times when you need to look a person in the eye:

1. When you say, "Thank you."
2. When you say, "I'm sorry."
3. When you're cursing someone out.

Never throw any of these over someone's shoulder.

4. If you're in the living room, don't ask me for chocolate ice cream when I'm in the kitchen. My ears are older than my teeth.

5. And while you're at it, you might as well call people "Sir" or "Ma'am." It doesn't hurt to do it, and you'd be surprised at how many people think you're polite if you can just stick a "Ma'am" at the end of the sentence.

What I'm saying is that you might as well be kind. It surprises the heck out of people. Give Sister Lil a hug when she gives you a D in Social Studies. You still won't get your iPad but you'll both feel a lot better.

In short, be more like Papa. Except when he's driving.

Aidan nodded. He's grown a lot this summer. Literally. Cracked the five-foot barrier last week, and I suspect that by Christmas I'll be the shortest Fisher-Paulson. Not much time before either high school or driving lessons, which I am certain Brian will not let me do.

Thus I wouldn't recommend motoring around the Outer, Outer, Outer, Outer Excelsior in the next two years. If you brake too quickly, some teenager's bound to roll down his window, look you in the eye and yell, "And all the bad words!"

Have It My Way

MY HUSBAND BRIAN, you may remember, only ever goes to four different restaurants, one of which must be Chinese. Won't try a new one until we've struck one off our list. This happens frequently, as the Fisher-Paulsons are what you might call *la bocce de mort* for San Francisco cuisine. We've killed off Yet Wah's, the Patio, Geneva Steak House, Cable Car Joe's. We go in, and the lights go out forever.

We're hoping that there's not a new murder mystery in the Outer, Outer, Outer, Outer Excelsior. On June 25 Bravo's closed its doors, and hasn't been seen again. We've tried calling, texting and even putting pizza on the back of a milk carton, but no answer. If Herb Caen had Moose's Grill, we had Bravo's.

But in the meantime, we tried substituting Hamburger Mary's in the Castro. A drag queen sat us down, then ignored our table for thirty-five minutes. Brian began his career on Broadway with *La Cage Aux Folles* and no one throws him shade. Bye Felicia.

So, we're down to three, my least favorite being my son Aidan's favorite: McDonald's. The only reason I give in is so we can play the Order-the-Food game.

It goes something like this: from the minute that the server asks, "How can I help you?" I rattle off the entire order without the possibility of a follow-up question:

"We'll have the Happy Meal six-piece Chicken McNuggets with the sauce for that being just ketchup, thank you very much, fries, extra salty, boy toy, a small chocolate shake with no whipped cream and no cherry, a cheeseburger with just cheese and burger, no onions, no pickles, and no secret sauces. Our family doesn't like secrets, especially in sauces, and no you don't want to hear that story. And one Big Mac without any beef. Yes, I know it comes with beef, and no, you will never catch me eating your so-called beef but since, unlike Burger King, you do not include a vegetarian alternative, I am forced to pay six bucks for three pieces of bread with lettuce and cheese because my son likes this place just to spite me, and no, nothing else, no drink, no dessert, no clown in yellow pantaloons, thank you very much. I will see you at the next window."

If the cashier asks me to repeat, I lose five points. If a follow-up question is asked, no matter what, the answer must be sung to the tune of "Hold the pickles, hold the lettuce."

We also play this game at Starbuck's, but not the one on Portola, where the baristas are psychic and know my order before I know my order.

Which leads us to the third place on Brian's list: Le P'tit Laurent. Aidan had an overnight which meant he wouldn't get mentioned in the column, saving me a couple of bucks. And it also meant we could have adult food.

As we walked in, the maître d' exclaimed, *"Monsieur Fisher! Bienvenue!"*

"He remembered our name," I said to Brian.

Brian smiled, "He remembered your name."

"As I recall, Fisher is your maiden name, not mine. And you're the famous dancer."

This bistro in Glen Park is the opposite of McDonald's. Riin, the waitress, always, always wins the Order-the-Food game. She has me at a disadvantage: she speaks real French, putting my three years of

Duolingo to shame. This means she understands the menu.

The other waiter speaks no French, which is a good thing for a French restaurant, so the two of us point and guess. But before I could say, "*Je voudrais*," Riin rifled off *Crème de Choux de Bruxelles* so fast that we ordered *Hachis Parmentier* and had *no* idea what was going to show up at the table.

When she asked, "*et pour boire?*" I pointed at "*Mauresque*," which ended up tasting like what would happen if you melted licorice and marzipan.

While we waited, I google translated *Hachis Parmentier* as 'Hatchets with Parmesan cheese' and thought we were in for the worst, but then came the dish, and Brian said, "Shepherd's Pie!" Or rather the high-class version: sausage and potatoes in a lyonnaise, each bite so warm and light that I finished my meal as well as Brian's.

I raised my *Mauresque*, Brian raised his *Sauvignon Blanc* and I toasted, as I always do, "To the best boys in the world."

And Brian replied, "Wherever they are."

Riin smiled. She knew we'd be back, if only to get another chance to win The Game, and because when we walked through the door, they would always say, "*Monsieur Fisher! Bienvenue!*"

Mishpocheh

WE CREATE when we choose family. And with the LGBTQ2 community, the family-making hasn't always been legal, so to us it's sacred.

My son Zane has a biological brother whom we didn't know about until the week that he got adopted by this very nice couple in Oakland. This was, by the way, the week that we adopted Aidan, and, yes indeed, Aidan has a biological brother who was adopted by a couple in Alameda. Aidan calls them the "logical" brothers, which implies, I suppose, that our own family is illogical.

Each of these brothers has an adoptive sister, so at first we had the problem of what does Zane call his adoptive brother Aidan's biological brother Adam's adoptive sister?

My husband Brian, a great believer in simplicity, said, "They're all cousins. We're all uncles. Except of course for the aunts."

The couple who raise Aidan's biological brother is Jewish and Chinese, so there are years we go from Hanukkah to Solstice to Christmas to Boxing Day to Kwanzaa to Lunar New Year without taking a breath. The Fisher-Paulson family tree has grown a fairly wide variety of fruits and nuts.

Thirteen years have passed, which means that last week was the day that Aidan's biological brother could say, "Today I am a man."

Believe it or not, with all the multi-culti in our family, I'd never been to a bar mitzvah.

My Jewish Inferiority Complex started back in Brooklyn (this was in the years between Ozone Park and the Outer, Outer, Outer, Outer Excelsior). Forty years ago, I had a Jewish boyfriend, and he kept saying I was "such a goy"— and he never said it like it was a good thing. One of his proofs was that I ate hamentashen three months after Purim. Another was that I didn't use hair conditioner.

So when Adam's father Larry invited us I was determined not to make a schlemiel of myself in front of my nephew. Last Saturday we drove out to Samuel Taylor State Park, somewhere in Marin, to its Redwood Grove. Immediately I bought into this Jewish liturgy, because if it was Catholic we'd have to dress up, and we wouldn't have gotten to see trees. Rabbi Mychal quoted John Muir, "The clearest way into the universe is through a forest."

Rabbi Mychal was untradial, as she is the first cleric I ever saw lead a service with a ukulele. We gathered with Adam's congregation under the shade of the Sequoias. Adam rang a gong.

Rabbi Mychal explained the one thing she wasn't going to do was ask Adam to say, "Today I am a man." Because growing up wasn't the point. No, the point was growing wise, and so at this ceremony he got to ask us questions. He asked what made us wake up in the morning, and then the Rabbi sent us to walk in the woods and find the divine because "to be spiritual is to be amazed."

Most of the others walked farther among the glades, but me I walked down to the stream with Aidan. This summer, while in Montana, he had mastered the art of rock skipping. I'd pretty much given up on discovering anything divine but I figured that I might as well get a picture of him. But the only way of getting a shot of his face was to cross the stream, so I took off my shoes and my socks, rolled up my jeans and started wading through the narrow waters.

Turns out there was a drop halfway, and — *kerplop* — I went waist deep into very cold water. It was then I had my realization:

that even when I think that I'm wading in the shallows, the divine is moving in the deep.

We gathered back in the circle, and it was time for Larry to bless his son. As he walked up, Larry looked me in the eye and began, "Kevin said something to me about ten years ago, and at the time I thought he didn't know what he was talking about, but today, I realize he was right. He said, 'Our children teach us.' Thank you, Adam, for teaching me, and I hope that you always ask the questions that make us wise."

Aidan still dry, me quite wet, I thought *Hmmm, maybe I should have let Aidan teach me a little harder.*

We drank wine, and we shared challah bread, and I thanked Larry for remembering me on this day that we celebrated his son.

Larry smiled and said, "After all, Kevin, we're *Mishpocheh;* family."

Yes, *Mishpocheh.* The *Mishpocheh* we create.

Extra Ordinary

JUST AN ordinary Monday, I went to pick up Aidan after work. Don't usually wear the star, uniform and gear home, but my husband Brian was on tour, and I was running late. Got out of the car, and I saw a guy with a dark mask running through the school parking lot, scaring the heck out of the kindergarteners. I used the big cop voice: "*STOP!*" and then gave chase. Officer Ahern from Ingleside swooped in at the same time, and we caught him.

The guy's excuse was that he had used the wrong drugs that day.

This was not *Dirty Harry*. This was not *Streets of San Francisco*. But Sister Lil and Ms. I, the assistant principals, were effusive. Father Agnel went so far as to write, "God sent him to be there at the right time and right place."

It's all well and good to have the nuns on my side but what I really wanted was my son's approval. I walked up the steps to the library, and Aidan looked up from the iPad long enough to shuffle to the car. As he turned the station from NPR to 99.7 NOW he asked, "Why were you so late picking me up?"

"Well, I stopped that man who was scaring the students."

"Oh."

"That it?" I asked. "No 'Good Job, Daddy'?"

Aidan shrugged again, clearly more interested in his iPad than this conversation. "Okay, if you really want one: Good Job, Daddy. But you know, this would be a brave thing if you were a mailman. For you this stuff is just… ordinary."

To him, twenty-five years as a deputy is just ordinary, but a decade or two before that I would have been considered ineligible.

Brian and I are just an ordinary couple, but thirty-two years ago we were the first gay men that any of our friends had ever seen get married. We didn't get any press coverage for inventing gay marriage because Al Gore hadn't invented the internet yet. The guy who was president at the time, Ronald Reagan — incidentally, the first divorcee to ever hold that office — said that ours was "an alternative lifestyle which I do not believe society can condone."

We didn't think we were revolutionaries on September 19, 1987, when the tape deck started playing "Here Comes the Groom." But ten years and two days later the United States Congress passed the Defense of Marriage Act, lest we destroy the sacred institution. It had been introduced by Congressman Bob Barr, who was on his third wife at the time.

We were domestically partnered on September 19, 1991 because Brian didn't want to remember another anniversary date.

We didn't think we were revolutionaries in 2003, when we applied to become foster parents. California had just recognized same-sex couple adoption formally, and it would still be illegal in many states for thirteen years. In that time, more than a hundred thousand other same-sex couples would adopt.

Crazy Mike once told me that you can protest in the streets all you want, but what really sells the revolution is when you're picking out china. No one thinks of us as the same-sex, mixed-race, mixed-preference family with rescue dogs on the block because by the time we did get legally married, on September 19, 2008 (because, again, Brian did not want to remember a new anniversary date), our San Francisco family was practically a cliché. Most of our neighbors in this cozy, foggy corner of the city think of us as the people who pay a mortgage on the Bedlam Blue Bungalow, fight with the school dis-trict, take the Kipcap in for a tune up, take Bandit to the vet. In short, we lead the most mundane of lives, but just ordinary is a miracle.

And on September 19, I am grateful to my husband for 21 years of illegal, and 11 years of legal wedded bliss. Thank you for the 34 Christmas trees, the 35 turkeys (we had an extra Thanksgiving one year), the 21 rescue dogs, the year with the triplets, the years with the 2 sons. Thank you for gathering those boys together every evening around the dining room table, saying grace and toasting, "The best boys in the world, wherever they are." But on this one night of the year we go out for dinner, and I toast the "The best husband in the world."

Our marriage, our family, is just like any other family you might find in the Outer, Outer, Outer, Outer Excelsior. Not extraordinary, but extra ordinary.

San Francisco Rules

Last week, President Trump did not visit San Francisco. Oh, he came close, but he doesn't have the courage to face us.

He hasn't left his heart in San Francisco. Whether he has a heart has been much speculated over, but not having visited since his election, he still feels free to say about our city, "They're in total violation — we're going to be giving them a notice soon."

Don't bother, Donald. In fact, let us put you on notice. This is the city of Saint Francis. We have our own rules:

1. You cannot fix complex problems with a sledgehammer. Bullying won't fix homelessness. These are individuals who live on the streets, humans with complex issues of addiction, income inequality and mental illness.

2. Never call it Frisco. If you insist on a nickname, use Frank.

3. We are all neighbors, whether the neighborhood is Nob Hill or the Outer, Outer, Outer, Outer Excelsior.

4. Yes, we are a city with flaws. But we own those flaws, and we learn from them. One of my readers, Mark Hetts, e-mails me every Thursday morning to tell me whether or not my column was a "clunker." For about a year, I lived in fear of getting that correspondence, until I realized that sometimes you gotta do something wrong before you can do it right. When asked about all of his experiments leading up to the light bulb, Edison said, "I have not failed. I've just found 10,000 ways that do not work."

5. We invented the martini, the fortune cookie, denim jeans, It's-Its, Irish Coffee, the juke box, television, and Rice-a-Roni. Here's what we know: there is always a solution. The story goes that William L. Murphy was courting a woman in 1932. She thought it was improper to visit a man's bedroom, but he lived in a one-room studio. So he invented a mattress that could be hidden in the wall frame, and now we call it the Murphy Bed. Don't ask me why Charles Hall invented the waterbed when he was a student in San Francisco State University in 1968... but Brian had one when we first started dating, and I was the only person in Jersey City to get seasick.

6. We try to know what we're talking about when we're talking. Or tweeting. What Trump said about the needles flowing into the oceans? That's why we have catch basins and treatment facilities. Matter of fact, let's talk trash. The average American produces about 4.4 pounds of waste a day, and the national standard is that only 34% gets recycled. And us? We recycle 80%. Not only do we invent. We re-invent.

7. We like the fog. Many call him Karl. I call her Karlotta. You've heard of gender-fluid? She's actually gender-vapor.

8. We celebrate random things. Where else could one of the most popular tourist sites be a former federal prison in the middle of a bay?

9. We cherish our history: the Gold Rush, the Barbary Coast, and even the earthquake. Couple hundred people get up at four in the morning every April to meet at Lotta's Fountain. Then we head over to Dolores Park to spray paint the water spigot that saved the Mission District. Do other cities gild their fire hydrants?

10. We cherish our future. Harvey Milk once said, "Hope will

never be silent." San Francisco is full of tomorrow. What makes it sweet is that, in this postage stamp city, we have the murals of Coit Tower, the TransAmerica Pyramid, the Seal Rock, the moan of the foghorn, the clang of the cable cars. And sometimes the beauty is a surprise: the three-story mural of the Woman's Building, the totem poles in Cayuga Park, the windmills just before you get to the Pacific Ocean.

11. We like our quirkiness. No other town has quite so many Sisters of Perpetual Indulgence.

12. Anne Herbert, who lived and died in the Bay Area, once said, "Practice random acts of kindness and senseless acts of beauty." *That* is what we are about here.

My son Aidan, at fourteen, has reduced this philosophy to what he calls "The Burrito Principle." If you're standing in line for any amount of time at La Coroneta for the best Mexican food in Glen Park, you might as well buy a burrito for the man who's sitting on the pavement outside.

Open your eyes, Mr. President, and while you're at it, open your wallet. When in doubt, use compassion.

If you ever do come to town, you'll see we don't build walls. We don't build cages. We build bridges, literally the Golden Gate.

Masquerade

THREE PARISH PRIESTS, seven psychiatrists, twenty-two therapists, thirty-seven social workers later, and the Fisher-Paulsons are still the craziest people in the Outer, Outer, Outer, Outer Excelsior.

From each one of these professionals we've gotten a trick or treat for how to cope with the modern family. These treats include: broadcast transitions; map out temperament; share power when able. Before Aidan even turned into a teenager, the professionals told us that he would always resist compromise.

The big trick comes when I complain that one of the boys has said, "I can't believe you're my adoptive father. What agency was dumb enough to license you?" The therapist will say, "Let's reframe this, shall we? Your son must feel really loved by you if he feels safe enough to say things like this."

So we reframe. The microwave that was set on fire is really just a chance to explore other cooking options. The failed math test is an opportunity for the family to spend quality time reviewing prime numbers. The fire alarm in the church was an exploration of response time for emergency service providers.

Nurse Vivian was not big on therapy, but she loved trick-or-treat. She did not believe in store-bought costumes; for her, that was the sartorial equivalent of Hamburger Helper. She started around August, asking what I wanted to be for Halloween. When she got home from swing watch at Jamaica Hospital, she'd be sewing that gypsy or pirate costume.

I regret that I wasn't grateful. The other boys and girls wore flashy rayon costumes with plastic masks, and I thought that was better. But 40 years later, I still have that handmade green velvet leprechaun costume (although any hope for my fitting in it ended, oh, about 39 years ago). She even sewed a half-black tuxedo/half-pink evening gown with spaghetti straps for me one year, and till his dying day, Hap attributed that costume to my lifestyle. Or half my lifestyle.

Not wanting to traumatize my own sons, each year I've asked them way in advance what they'd like to dress up as for Halloween. Zane was always low maintenance: whatever superhero film we watched that year. I've dressed the boys as Green Lantern and Flash, Batman and Robin, Iron Man and Hulk, Superman and Superboy, Captain America and Bucky Barnes, Black Panther and Ant Man.

But by last Halloween, Zane was gone across the desert and over the mountain. Aidan abandoned our motif and went instead for high concept. He asked for this dinosaur that included a battery-powered fan that blew it up and allowed him to make realistic dinosaur noises. (How did anyone know what a dinosaur really sounded like? Did they use 8-track tapes then?)

$250 later we had the deluxe Tyrannosaurus Rex. I left for work, and before I ever saw him in it, Aidan had managed to sell his costume to a sixth-grader. Maybe it was because I missed Zane, but it was the worst Halloween ever.

Thus, when gourd season came upon us this year, I asked, "Who do you want to be for Halloween? And by 'want to be' I do not mean purchasing another high-end costume that you make a profit off of."

"Slender Man."

"Who's Slender Man?"

Eye roll. "From Minecraft."

Of course, I looked it up. This dude was creepy. The Slender Man was a creature of the internet, created by Eric Knudsen. He has no face and wears a black suit, and the stories feature him stalking, abducting and otherwise traumatizing children.

Being a responsible parent, I countered, "OK, so do you want to be Spiderman or Doctor Strange?"

"Slender Man," he replied.

This went on for weeks until my husband Brian went on tour. Aidan wanted a banana split from Mitchell's for dinner and knew I wouldn't budge unless he gave in on something big.

"Fine," he said, "I'll be Thanos."

Before Aidan had finished his grasshopper pie, the deluxe version was ordered, complete with infinity gauntlet.

Brian flew home the next day, so that night I said, "We won! He's getting a Thanos costume!" My fist raised, waiting for his bump.

"OK, you didn't want him to be a serial killer, so instead you went with the Marvel villain who snapped his fingers and murdered half of the beings in the universe..."

"Brian, let's reframe that, shall we? He's gone from bogeyman of the World Wide Web to the one guy who could take out the Avengers. It demonstrates he has some ambition. And also, Aidan compromised."

Brian gave me a tepid fist bump, raised his wine glass and said, "To Aidan, Super Villain of the Year."

Sweaters in the Fridge

MY HUSBAND Brian dances with several different modern dance companies, which means he does a fair amount of touring. Whenever we drive Brian to the airport for one of these excursions, my son Aidan sits in the back seat of the Kipcap. When we pull over at departures, Aidan says with that sweet little voice, "I'm gonna miss you, Papa." But it's not true. Aidan's a shrewd businessperson. He's read a lot more books on childing than I've ever read on parenting. He knows that if Papa's away for more than three days, he gets a t-shirt or a stuffed wolf.

He also knows I'm the more easily intimidated parent, and so I give in to the dinner at Mitchell's Ice Cream (or as we know it, Sundae Monday) or staying up till midnight watching *Teen Titans Go!*

This week, before Brian has another tour, Juan, one of the ex-dancers in Sean Dorsey Dance, will get married at City Hall. Another thing to love about this city: it's blasé to go to a gay wedding. If I say I'm going to a queer vegan broom-jumping, no one blinks. The only question I got was, "Was the broom organic?"

To which I answer, "No but it's kosher."

No, if you want exotic in San Francisco, go to a Catholic Wedding.

In San Francisco City Hall, the building with the highest rotunda dome in the nation, we see hoop skirts on an hourly basis but my favorite this year were the groom and groom who dressed as the *Superman/Aquaman Hour of Adventure*.

Whenever we are invited, Brian and I always buy the couple a pair of champagne flutes. The two of us are older than gay marriage itself, and when we got hitched, no one let us into a bridal registry, so we bought ourselves a set of two Powerscourt champagne flutes, and began, what would become over 34 years, a service for eight of Noritake Virtue and Waterford. By 50, we'll have the silverware.

Aidan is not good at changes in routine, so us attending a reception had him in a tizzy. As soon as Brian left, he asked, "I don't get this whole marriage thing. Daddy, why would you ever marry someone like Papa?"

The truth of the matter? I made a lousy bachelor. Brian saved me from a lifetime of sweaters in the refrigerator.

I haven't been single since 1985. Reagan was in office and I lived in a two-room flat in Hoboken, the mile square city. Not every city can be San Francisco.

I worked long hours at Macy*s, then long nights at the AIDS crisis line, which is to say that I was in that apartment long enough to sleep.

The only heat was from the stove, so I baked a lot of brownies in the winter, and that was about the only cooking I did. You think that it'll be fun being single because you can pick whatever you want to eat but what you really get is a lot of Ramen noodles.

The only advantage of single life was that I got to use the express lane at the supermarket. And because I never cooked more than a shelf's worth of food, I stored my sweaters in the refrigerator.

Dating was never fun for me because at some point I ran out of small talk. One guy broke up with me because I didn't use hair conditioner, another guy because of those sweaters in the fridge.

Could have been worse — in ancient Greek times, if you got to the age of 21 in Sparta and still weren't married, you had to walk naked through the marketplace singing a song about your dishonor.

Amanda, who even knew me back then (in the 80s, I mean, not ancient Greece), and who partied a lot more, insisted, "Kevin, you're already a spinster." She may have been more adventurous than me, having dated everyone from a gun moll to a circus clown, but Amanda never spent her Saturday nights doing needlepoint.

Thus when I met Brian over that fateful lasagna dinner I was ready to give up my nights of wanton debauchery.

Didn't hurt that I fell in love.

"Some day, Aidan, you're gonna get married. You won't live in a house. You'll live in a home. Very much like we do in the Bedlam Blue Bungalow in the Outer, Outer, Outer, Outer Excelsior. And here's the best part: after all the fireworks, you will know exactly who you're having dinner with every night. You'll sit at the kitchen table, and hold hands and say grace and someday, you'll toast "the best boys in the world.""

To which Aidan answered, "Wherever they are."

Helicopter Parenting

FLEET WEEK: every year a Chief Deputy gets invited to fly out by helicopter to meet the United States Navy as they sail into the harbor. As I'm the most senior chief never to have done this, my boss gave me first dibs, but alas my husband had a rehearsal and that left no one to watch Aidan.

Crazy Michele went instead, and she represented the San Francisco Sheriff's Department better than I would have, although I do have a stronger interest in sailors.

She learned a few things in that chopper:
1. If you don't duck, you can lose your head.
2. You're probably not gonna see it coming when something bad happens.
3. You have to fly low to fly safe, but that presents its own danger.

Ironically while she was flying over the Pacific, I was helicopter parenting in the Outer, Outer, Outer, Outer Excelsior.

Dr. Haim Ginott coined the term "helicopter parent" in 1969 and it was intended as a pejorative, but I think of it as a badge of honor.

My mother, Nurse Vivian, had been a helicopter parent since Leonardo da Vinci designed the aerial screw. Oh, not with me. With Brother X. When Brother X got held back in the second grade, Sister Mary Magdalen recommended that he go to a psychiatrist because Brother X couldn't even tie his own shoes.

The psychiatrist asked, "Don't you know how to tie your shoes?"

Brother X replied, "Why should I? She does it for me."

Six years later, when I was entering kindergarten, Nurse Vivian, a little older, a little wiser, advised, "You'd better learn to tie your own shoes. Either that or save up for loafers."

Crazy Mike wanted me to write about Zane this week, but that's not how it worked out. He got me to thinking whether I had failed to helicopter Zane. What if I hadn't let the school district bully us into Thurgood Marshall?

My son went over the mountains and across a prairie and I'm left with "Satellite Image Parenting." We get two ten-minute telephone conversations a week, and it feels like a theoretical son. He's taller than me now, and the timbre of his voice lowers with each call.

So I over-compensate. Since Zane went away, Aidan's life looks like the opening montage of MASH: helicopters everywhere.

Whirlybird wisdom: Don't read the parenting books. They're gonna tell you that if you protect your child, she/he's never going to win an Olympic medal or get into Harvard. And all this is very good if you have a Stepford child, but since I've been writing this column, I've found there are a lot more parents with spirited children than there are parents with straight-A students. Let me tell you this: you leave a spirited child alone for fifteen minutes, you'll be cleaning peanut butter and jelly sandwiches out of your furnace vent.

If you have a spirited child, you darn well better helicopter. If you don't, you're going to spend your Indigenous People's Day Weekend with 32 homework assignments undone.

Eighth grade. Don't believe the hype. This is the killing zone. Parents who smile and say, "Oh, I let little Bobby choose between the glockenspiel and the sousaphone," will suddenly become "Torpedo Parents." And high school selection is proof that Darwin was right: survival of the fittest means getting into SI.

But us, we're not trying for Lowell or Lick Wilmerding. We're just seeking to keep the young one out of reform school.

Which brings me to Aidan's pal. Let's call him J. Now, his mother believes in "Remote Control Parenting." She set up a webcam in her house. And it's true that little J can tie his own shoelaces, whereas Aidan never unties his shoes. He just squeezes in and out of them. Last week J's mom said, "Hey, I know it's a school night, but we've got tickets for the Warriors practice at the Chase Center. Can Aidan come?"

I hesitated but I agreed.

She picked them up from St. John's on a Monday night. Sister Lil was shocked. Tia Ana, the woman who runs the after-school program asked, "You're okay with this?"

"Okay" is a strong word. But it's been a year or so since the head stuck in the staircase. The pencils in the microwave. The magnets in the sewage line.

Crazy Michele may be smart enough not to have children, but what she said of the helicopter is also true of parenting: You have to fly low to fly safe, but that presents its own danger.

A Letter Home

A JOURNEY of a thousand miles begins with a single limo ride to Fisherman's Wharf.

Sister Shirley called me on Monday to ask whether I could chaperone the eighth graders on Tuesday. I asked why not invite Brian to go instead, and Sister Shirley replied, "They're eighth graders. The chaperone either has to be a nun, or someone like a nun."

Have I mentioned that the maiden name of my mother, Nurse Vivian, was Wise? Whenever she gave us advice, she would start with "A word to the Wise." About this she said, "You can disagree with the parish priest. In fact, you'd better. They're a little too full of themselves. But you'd better do exactly what a nun tells you." So, I took Tuesday afternoon off.

As field trips go, this was an easy one. The top sellers of See's chocolate in the annual fundraiser were invited to lunch at In-N-Out Burger in Fisherman's Wharf, and we drove down in a limo.

The first place I ever visited in San Francisco was the wharf, and to a tourist it feels like magic: the smell of crabs and salmon, the cool mist blowing in over Alcatraz, the foghorn moaning, Ghirardelli's Chocolate, the tall spire of Coit Tower gleaming in the background.

In a city where even the garbage is complicated, it's easy to forget its charm. But the Wharf has not changed. It still sells snow globes filled with cable cars. And with eighth graders, there's a sense of wonder. Through their eyes I saw what little miracles there are in the holiday tree being put up and the sea lions and the Maxfield Parrish clouds.

And as part of that miracle there were these persons who I had known since they sang at the Nativity scene in the first grade. But little Jelly was now Anjelica. RJ, who kicked his soccer cleats off into the air instead of the ball every single game, was now Roberto. Voices were cracking, little whispers appearing over their lips, but I was lucky enough to still be Coach Kevin. Like San Francisco, I was one of those things that didn't change while everything changed around them.

That week, Aidan and I had his first class for Confirmation (think of it as Bar Mitzvah-lite). As usual, Sister Lil had more advice for the parents than she did for the teenagers. She said that this sacrament meant that the relationship between the parent and the offspring was changing, most especially in how the two generations spoke to each other.

"Your young men and women," she said, "will stop asking you questions that you can answer and will start asking you questions that no one can answer. The second thing is the way that they listen. It will appear that they will not hear a word you say, no matter whether you repeat it three times or thirty times, then one day, you will learn they've been sitting in the back seat, the entire trip, listening."

Longtime readers of this column know that my oldest son Zane went a thousand miles away over the mountains and across the prairies on a pilgrimage to find himself. A candle continues to burn in the window to show him the way back to the Bedlam Blue Bungalow in the Outer, Outer, Outer, Outer Excelsior, but there are a lot of nights I wonder what it was that I did not say, whether or not I gave him enough wisdom. Should I have said it thirty times? Thirty times thirty?

My husband Brian mails Zane a letter every week. We sit around the table on Sunday morning, and we each write a note, and Brian puts a copy of the column in the envelope, to let Zane know that everything changes around him, but my Dad jokes remain the same.

Zane rarely comments about his clipping from the Voice of the West. And he never writes home. Occasionally, another boy in the group will say, "Nice column, Mr. Kevin!" so I know someone out there is getting little doses of my wisdom.

But we came home that night of Sister Lil's class, and there was a letter from Montana:

"I know what I have to do now. I need to learn to do the right things, even when no one's looking. I hope to one day walk through the door to our house with my bags and say, '*Dad, we all go on journeys, but some take longer than others to find their way back home.*'

Love, Zane"

Unanswerable

M ANY READERS don't know that I don't have a Datebook address. This isn't a complaint because my brain doesn't have room for one more password. But the upshot is that some mysterious person forwards the e-mails, sometimes on the same day, sometimes within a few weeks. Sometimes in clumps, like the day I got 812. I make a point of answering all missives, from my citizen's e-mail address. A few people, like Jean Sward, reply back over and over and become extended family because God knows my sons Zane and Aidan can use a few more aunts and uncles.

Jean wrote to find out what I meant last week about "teenagers asking questions that have no answer." You'd have to live with Aidan full time to get it. Try driving him to school. It takes about forty-five minutes for his medication to kick in, so during that one short drive to St. John's School he sits in the back seat, just waiting until Brian is about to curse out a driver/pedestrian/traffic light when he queries, "Who's faster: the Flash or God?"

Other questions while driving in the Kipcap:

Upon seeing the Sheriff's Department bus driving up 280 north: Do jail buses have emergency exits?

Does a hearse get to use the carpool lane?

Now sometimes he's asking: "What's the dive speed of a peregrine falcon?" but he knows the answer: 200 mph. He's sitting there with the book. But he asks to find out whether or not his Dad is still omniscient. So I answer with a question myself: "How could the boy who couldn't read his one assigned chapter of *To Kill a Mockingbird* possibly be able to memorize the *Encyclopedia of Raptors*?"

Some questions are judgments. Since June 25, when our beloved Bravo's closed its doors for the last time, I've been unable to enter another pizza parlor. We got as far as Little Joe's, right across the street, and I couldn't make my foot walk through the door. Aidan put his arm on my shoulder: "I guess we're not ready to move on?"

His follow-up question, when the delivery man arrived was: "Why do they put round pizza into a square box?" The answer: they ran out of triangles.

Some questions are just random:

At the Century 20 movie theater: "Which arm rest is yours?"

We'd gone to Hollister's in the Serramonte Mall to get a birthday present for his friend (son of Sasb). As the clerk rang up an over-priced ombre shirt, she asked, "Would you like us to put you on the mailing list?"

I demurred, "This really isn't my style."

To which she persisted, "We put grandparents on all the time." I probably could have borne that until Aidan queried, "Daddy, if you were a couch, would you be an antique?"— followed, a little more soberly by, "Daddy, are you old enough to die of old age?"

If a clowder of cats jump on top of each other, is it still a dog-pile? In case you're wondering about that clowder term, he also memorized the collective nouns for predators.

In a library, do they put the Bible in the fiction or nonfiction section?

Some questions must have an answer, but need a brighter person than Daddy:

If the antonym of synonym is antonym, what is the synonym for synonym?

Aidan does not ask rhetorical questions, which to him means that the asker doesn't really expect to hear an answer, i.e. "Who put all the pencils in the microwave?" No, he leaves that to Daddy. Instead he asks, unrhetorically, "What is the term for a question that has no answer?"

I asked Crazy Mike this and he said, "There is no such thing as a question that has no answer. All questions, like all prayers, have an answer."

Sister Lil (her rap name is Lil Sister) responded to that: "God always answers prayers, but humans don't always listen."

Aidan persists: Why do you keep telling me not to take candy from strangers, but let me go trick or treating?

What is the speed of dark?

If we make angel cake, do angels make people cake?

If the package on a stick of gum says 50 calories per piece, is that for chewing the gum or swallowing it?

Aidan shakes his head when I cannot answer, and I can only quote Mark Twain: "When I was a boy of 14, my father was so ignorant I could barely stand to have the old man around. But when I got to be 21, I was astonished at how much the old man had learned in seven years."

Broken Holiday

I DIDN'T REALIZE IT at the time, but 1975 was the last year that the Paulson family gathered as one for Thanksgiving: Nurse Vivian, Hap, Brother X, Brother XX, Whiskers and me. I went off to Notre Dame the next year, and began the first of my Orphan Thanksgivings, which are also sweet, but never as sweet as Nurse Vivian's apple pie.

First it was college, and the chapel choir gathered at Professor Seid-Martin's home, lots of salads, the first glass of wine for most of us.

Orphan Thanksgivings are how I learned to create family. By the time I met my husband Brian in 1985, I knew that whoever we broke bread with that day made for a bond of sorts, a bond that got renewed as we toasted to the gratitude we felt. Anything we did three years in a row became tradition.

In our thirty-five years, we've only missed one together, the year Nurse Vivian got sick.

Since moving into the Bedlam Blue Bungalow in the Outer, Outer, Outer, Outer Excelsior twenty years ago, we have hosted each year, and each year created more family. There are only four persons in the world with the name Fisher-Paulson, but if you looked at our dining room table, you'd think it was in the hundreds.

Until a year and a half ago, Zane and Aidan had spent each holiday under our roof. I thought that it would always be that way, but then Zane went over the mountains and across the prairie, and a holiday was lost. So when they told us that he could visit this November, I wanted the day to be perfect.

What are the odds of a cracked tooth, a fractured windshield, a broken arm and a torn ACL all happening the week before the visit? Just ask the Fisher-Paulsons. If you put our month to music, you would have a bad country music song.

Worst part for Aidan was that he didn't even get a good story out of his busted wing. Other people will get back from break telling tales of snowboarding or skydiving. His arm broke because I was inept, and held onto his wrist when I should have let go. Aidan took it in stride though, and now has a bionic humerus. His arm only hurts when one of us suggests homework.

Speaking of clumsy, things not to hear during dental surgery: "Ooops!" as in, while Dear Doctor Robyn was wrestling with my broken bicuspid, she popped the top right off of my molar. Doctor Robyn said, "You need a new crown."

And I said, "I know, right." As Brian always says, "I just love new ways to wear gold."

Buddyboy, alas, has no story for his torn anterior cruciate ligament, so we've been telling people he did it on his floor routine in the canine Olympics. So Buddyboy got "the cone of shame" instead of a crown. (We told Aidan he needed to wear a cone for his broken arm, but he wasn't having it.)

This led to what my husband Brian called "The Thanksgiving *des Invalides*."

Thus it was no surprise that when Zane landed at SFO, his luggage did not land with him.

But still we gathered: Maureen and Maya, the girl next door who has never celebrated Thanksgiving anywhere other than with us, the Ottavianos, who also have a son who went over the mountains, Uncle Doya, Uncle Jon, Aunt Dee and Uncle Howard. Fifteen of us gathered around the three mismatched tables in our dining room, and before grace we named our gratitude, and then toasted "the best children in the world."

Southern fried corn, asparagus and cheese casserole, quinoa stuffed squash and brined turkey, followed by a dozen pies.

Here's what we learned: it doesn't matter how imperfect the holiday is. It doesn't matter if it happens in Ozone Park or the Outer, Outer, Outer, Outer Excelsior. It doesn't matter that the spilled blackberry pie in the oven set off the smoke detector. It doesn't matter that Faith put the pumpkin pie at a level at which Bandit could lick the custard out. (But not Buddyboy... alas, he wore the cone of shame.)

It doesn't matter that at the end of the weekend, Zane will go over the mountains and across the prairies. Here's what matters: he will come back.

Here's what matters: teeth, arm bones and windshields, and yes, even traditions may get broken when the bread gets broken, but the holiday remains whole. Each of us in our own way is an orphan, and what makes us family is the choice to be together.

Apostrophes, Shrieks and Interrobangs

THE COLUMN I wrote a few years ago about the Harvard Comma got me quite a lot of. . . well you wouldn't call it "hate mail" so much as "disdain mail." Grammarians wrote about its sacrosanct quality, correcting me that it wasn't even the Harvard comma, but the Oxford comma.

Granted I didn't go to an Ivy League college. Harvard writers waste perfectly good commas by putting them before the word "and." At Notre Dame, we American Studies majors realized that in the American language, as opposed to the English one, punctuation is more a matter of style. Thus, we have the Notre Dame Exclamation point! There's a big difference between, "Harvard won the game," which is fiction, and "The Fightin' Irish won!!!" which is divine providence. With the Crimsons, the exclamation point is useful only for mathematical factorials, whereas at Notre Dame, we're just enthusiastic.

F. Scott Fitzgerald, who attended Princeton (which is a lot like Harvard, only in New Jersey) wrote, "Cut out all those exclamation marks. An exclamation mark is like laughing at your own jokes." What Fitzgerald failed to realize is that sometimes your own joke is funny. And he also failed to realize he was in America, because, whereas the Brits call it an exclamation mark, we call it an exclamation point.

Wasn't always a thing. Started out with Latin, where the word for joy was "io" and the I was written above the O, and this symbol mutated, in the 15TH century or so, into the exclamation point.

This is how old I am. Growing up in South Ozone Park, I didn't even have an exclamation point on my typewriter. I had to type a period, then go back and type an apostrophe above it. No, don't go saying that the Paulsons were so poor they couldn't afford an exclamation point. Wasn't until 1970 that it caught on with typewriters.

In the days of newspaper typesetters, the exclamation point was called the shriek. And in the days of the old Dictaphones, executives would say the word "bang" when they wanted an exclamation point, which is why to this day if you put a question mark together with an exclamation point it's called an interrobang?!

You'll notice that it's not the Fighting Irish, but rather the Fightin' Irish. Back to style: we Domers know how to spell, but the apostrophe indicates that when we're talking Women's Basketball or Football, no one bothers to pronounce that 'g' right before Irish.

Which brings me to John Richards, who wrote, "With regret I have to announce that, after some 18 years, I have decided to close the Apostrophe Protection Society… fewer organisations and individuals are now caring about the correct use of the apostrophe in the English Language… the ignorance and laziness present in modern times have won!"

Poor Mr. Richards and his 257 members. He missed the point that grammar should be fun, not work. For the record, here are the Do's and Don'ts of Using the Apostrophe:

1. It's used for omissions, in "He'll go to hell!"
2. It's used for possessives, thus "The dog's toy is in the bedroom." The only tricky part of this is that if you have more than one dog, then the apostrophe goes after the s, as in "The dogs' toy is in the bedroom." For the record, Buddyboy and Bandit do not share toys, such as Mr. Rope, thus this sentence makes no sense to them. The only tricky part of this

tricky part is that if a noun ends in an s or a z you don't add an s, so if I used my middle name, I would say, "Thaddeus' car is the Kipcap."

3. It's used for the plurals of single letters as in "The good news is that Aidan's report card had more D's than it did F's."

I mentioned two weeks ago that the first collection of my columns had come out (*How We Keep Spinning...!*). What I did not mention was the argument. My husband Brian read the manuscript and moved the periods inside parenthetical remarks. The revisions went to my editor Patrick, who reinserted them. We went through about five cycles before I announced, "The Outer, Outer, Outer, Outer Excelsior is now the Switzerland of punctuation."

And there you have it. We Fisher-Paulsons may not know how to use the other thirteen punctuation marks (period, comma, colon, semi-colon, question mark, the en dash, the em dash, hyphen, bracket, brace, parentheses, quotation mark and ellipsis,) but we sure do know how to use the exclamation point!!!!!!!!!!

Yes, Zanebug

In 1897, Doctor Philip O'Hanlon's daughter, Virginia, asked him whether or not Santa Claus existed. He told her to write to the The Sun because "If you see it in the newspaper, it's so."

122 years later, this is unlikely to work as a parenting strategy. My son Aidan reads the newspaper only to see how many times his name gets mentioned.

But Virginia did write, and one of the editors, Francis Pharcellus Church, responded. Ironically for a guy named Church, he was a devout atheist. But here's an excerpt:

"...Yes, Virginia, there is a Santa Claus. He exists as certainly as love and generosity and devotion exist, and you know that they abound and give to your life its highest beauty and joy... not believe in Santa Claus! You might as well not believe in fairies!"

It's hard to believe in what you cannot see.

My son Zane visited in November. He was loving and funny. He said that he read my new book (*How We Keep Spinning...!*) on the airplane, and that it was even better than the Justice League. He even let Aidan beat him at Uno.

But Zane went back over the mountains and across the prairie and he will not be home for Christmas. For the second year he'll miss the cinnamon buns. He'll miss the roof cow wearing antlers. Tom and Jerry's giant tree on 21ST Street. Midnight mass at Most Holy

Redeemer. He'll miss the Talling of the Boys.

The thing about Christmas is that it's a great time to feel sad. But I've got my husband Brian and Aidan to commiserate with.

We've made no plans for the holidays except that we'll light the menorah with Aidan's Jewish brother, because Hanukah is about striking a match against all odds. The miracle is not that the candle keeps burning, but that we've gathered together to witness.

Then we'll have the ornament party, and we'll gather around the piano, and I guarantee that I'll start crying when Uncle Quentin plays "I'll Be Home for Christmas." We've got no plans for Christmas Eve or Christmas Day, and I'm okay with that. Maybe even relieved.

But Zane is in Montana, with boys like him.

We got a call on Wednesday that he had acted out. Not at all surprising. So we talked on the phone, and he owned what he did, but the hardest part was him saying, "Some days I think I'll never get home."

Each week, this column gets turned in by Friday afternoon: good, bad or clunker. It comes out the following Wednesday, and Susan, a fellow Sheriff's employee, cuts it out of the newspaper so I have a copy to mail to Zane.

Thus I'm writing this last part of the column to my son, and Susan will give it to me on the 18th, and I hope that he'll be reading it by Christmas Eve.

Dear Zane,

It's easy to get things confused because Christmas is not the things you see on Hallmark. It's not the snow. It's not Krispy Kremes turning from the pumpkin-filled to the gingerbread donut. It's not the new bike with a shiny bow.

It's not about the gifts you get but about the gifts you give. Christmas is messy, just like family is messy.

We Catholics focus on the Madonna but the past few years I've been thinking a lot about Joseph, shivering in the cold, off to stage left in the nativity scene. He's in a barn. He's taking care of a son not his own. Shepherds are walking up to him talking about stars and kings.

But Joseph doesn't know what's going on. No angel has clued him in. They flee to another country, and Joseph has no idea how his adopted son will turn out. On the journey, Joseph protects him and speaks to him his truths.

I get it now. Christmas has always been about a father being scared, and a son going out into the desert because he has a wonderful but daunting destiny. And somehow the son comes back. And family endures.

Yes, Zanebug, there is a way home. There is a shining city on the hill, tucked away in the fog, and that city believes in you. Not believe in coming home! You might as well not believe in Fisher-Paulsons! In all the world there is nothing more real than the fact that you are always coming home to us, and one day you will arrive.

Next year in San Francisco.

Love,

Dad

A Boxing Day Miracle

ZANE IS HOME. For a while, at least. The journey away has always been a circle, has always been the way back, a pilgrimage to the Outer, Outer, Outer, Outer Excelsior. Column doesn't need any more than that, but for those of you who want the other 722 words, here it is:

The Fisher-Paulsons don't believe in wasting a perfectly good crisis. Week before Christmas the director of the school stated that Zane could come back as soon as we could arrange the travel. Sounded like she was over the Fisher-Paulsons, but we take what we can get. She doubted we could get a flight this close to the holiday. Just tap your heels together and say, "There's no place like home." This is our son, and Alaska airlines took mercy on us, and there, the Saturday before Christmas, five hours after the plane was due, our son arrived in SFO. His suitcase took a day or two more, but you got to have a few flaws. Still and all, I felt like George Bailey in the last reel of *It's a Wonderful Life*, with Brian (as Mary) running in, saying, "Oh, George. It's a miracle."

We didn't expect Zane back before Easter, and here he was in time for the Ornament Party. The neighborhood knows it's the season because our outdoor nativity gets turned on and the whole *tableau vivant* stays lit until the Feast of the Magi. Or until we take it down, which some years doesn't happen til President's Day.

The ornament party. Comes from my Ozone Park Days, when every family on the Irish block decorated everyone else's tree, including the Carbones. Ours was the last home, and by that time more than a few Presbyterians had been consumed, and so our plastic tree was always just a little crooked. Ornaments got mixed up in the process, so our modern adaptation is: You walk in the door with an ornament. You walk out the door with a different ornament.

As regular readers know, the house down the hill from us has a cow on the roof, and her owners (John and Susan) come to the soiree, threatening to trade out one of our blow mold figures so that we would have the only two-Joseph crèche in all of Christendom. They're looking for some lesbian Catholics who want to trade for a second virgin. That and replacing the Star of Bethlehem with a disco ball. But it didn't matter if we had the three kings or three stooges; our son was home.

And that night, the solstice, and the first night feast of the festival of light in the Jewish tradition, Aidan's 'logical brother' Adam lit the candles and said, "Blessed are you…Who made miracles in those days at this time." And I knew it wasn't just a Christmas miracle but a Hanukah Miracle as well.

What's more, it was a Boxing Day Miracle. A Talling-of-the-Boys Day miracle. New Year's Day has never been big for us. We make cinnamon rolls in the morning, the simple kind that come in a can, and after we eat, we stand the boys up by the bathroom door and find out how they've grown. Only there was a blank spot last year. So the not-so-little joy was to find that Aidan has made it all the way up to 5'2 ½" and Zane is 5'10 ½", **OFFICIALLY** taller than his Dads. Other parents have warned me that this means he'll no longer take me quite so seriously.

There's a downside to Zane being back. Now it will cost me five bucks to mention either one of them. Zane's saving up for a phone.

Zane is still a boy with challenges. We're still a family with challenges. He's changed. But not completely. How much is just being a teenager? How much does any father know?

Every once in a while, Crazy Mike accuses me of not having a point to the story. Or at least not making the point clear. So let me say this: the Law of Entropy dictates that everything falls apart. Families break in pieces, and sons get lost and dogs sit at the door waiting for their boy to come home.

And most of us don't get burning bushes or seas divided in two or even our neighbors showing up with $8000 and a bottle of wine. Here's what we get: our son comes home earlier than expected. The ordinary is the miracle, when a family holds together in a way that can only be called love. For right now the Bedlam Blue Bungalow has a lot more tails wagging than it has had in a year and a half.

But the story is not over. This is not a happy ending. More like a happy middle.

Feast of Nothing Special

THIS PAST SUNDAY, Father Matt stopped wearing white and went back to the everyday green vestments. We Catholics hang onto Christmas for a long time, but even my husband Brian takes the tree down at some point. The electric nativity has been stored in the garage, the stockings have been unhung from the chimney with care and even the Roof Cow down the block is naked. I told John and Susan they should at least cover her udders with a fig leaf, but Susan replied, "Even roof cows take a holiday from the holidays."

It will take a few more weekends to dismantle Brian's Christmas Village/Megalopolis, but even in the Outer, Outer, Outer, Outer Excelsior, we are in what liturgical calendars call "Ordinary Time."

Today is the feast of Saint Ceolwulph. There's a reason you never heard of him. He's the patron saint of Nothing Special, so it's unlikely that you're going to name your firstborn after him.

Growing up in Ozone Park, I wanted Christmas to last all year but now I see why we need a break. It's why we have ten months of school followed by two months of summer. It's why we have four months of basketball followed by one month of March Madness, which inexplicably occurs in April. We need a break from the extraordinary and the Fisher-Paulsons love ordinary because we get so little of it. I asked Brian what he wanted for a gift and he told me "Twenty minutes without a crisis."

And thus, we are in the mundane. Aidan's cast has been removed, and for Zane the unified school district picked the high school in the city farthest from the Bedlam Blue Bungalow: Washington High. We Fisher-Paulsons are notorious and first day out, the assistant principal, Ms. Lynch, understood that their names were a lot more likely to get mentioned in the newspaper.

Last week I read from my new book, *How We Keep Spinning...!* at Green Apple Books. As Zane and I drove across town, I worried, "The first week that we moved to San Francisco, I walked into Gump's, and it happened to be the day that Herb Caen was reading. The room was full. Me, I hope that somebody shows up. I'm going to be really embarrassed if we're the only ones."

Zane mused. "People will show up. You're the Carlisle."

"Who?"

He rolled his eyes, and explained, "Carlisle. In *Breaking Dawn*."

"The wimpy vampire."

"I mean the guy that everybody shows up for. The guy who when you get killed the rest of us go berserk."

We parked the Kipcap and walked into the store. I was wrong. Zane was right. Eileen, the manager, said, "You must be better known than I thought. Yesterday, I never heard of you. Today, the room's already full. We sold out of your books. Some woman even left a cake."

I'm not at all famous, but Eileen was right about one part, I do inspire carbohydrates in others. Dianne Boate had left a sour cream pound cake with lemon glaze, frosting and a peanut brittle garnish. What even Dianne didn't know was that at the exact same moment, Rodney Anderson, having figured out the location of the Bedlam Blue Bungalow, was leaving Bravo's Pizza at our door. I haven't been able to go in there since the restaurant reopened under a new owner, so Rodney volunteered to be my canary in the pizza parlor.

But back to Green Apple: even though the evening was crowded, we had a lot of fun. The reading room was indeed full, so I walked through the aisles, reading from the book, delighted that I was on a first name basis with so many people in this wonderful city, tethered to the shoreline by only the fog. My sons Zane and Aidan, having reasoned that this related to the San Francisco Chronicle, invoked the Leah Garchik rule: every time their name was mentioned they got $5. So, they walked through the aisle, taking selfies, and more people wanted their autograph than mine. And even though I lost money, it seemed only right. This is their journey.

There will be more readings, and we would love to see you there. Just don't mention Zane or Aidan's name.

It's not likely that the event will be overcrowded, but remember that if I get snuffed, all the other vampires will go berserk.

Midnight with Crazy Mike

CRAZY MIKE and I first met on October 8, 1998. The coincidence was that I had met Brian on October 8, 1985, and so I shared the same anniversary with my husband as I did my beat wife.

October 8, 1998 was my first night as a sergeant, and Crazy Mike was a senior deputy, my second-in-command. We worked on midnight watch at a tiny jail which no longer even exists as a jail anymore. We hit it off because he put Karen Carpenter's "There's No Place Like Home for the Holidays" on in the control room. I asked him why Richard Carpenter never sang and we decided that there were two seasons for music: Christmas from the Vernal Equinox until Epiphany, and contraltos singing show tunes for the rest of the year.

He worked a lot of overtime because he was buying his wife a burial niche in a columbarium for Christmas. He did not think this odd and neither did Mrs. Crazy Mike. His card read, "Now you CAN leave your heart in San Francisco, as well as other organs...."

Crazy Mike loved graveyard shift, probably because his progeny were teenagers at the time, and it was a way to avoid them. But I could never get the rhythm of it down. Each night as I drove through the fog of Skyline Boulevard, it was like descending into a dream, and I fought to stay awake. Some nights that meant memorizing long poems, some nights studying Japanese, and once, I challenged each of the six pod deputies to a game of Scrabble, walking from one to the next, winner take the Boston Cream pie in the Officer's Dining Room. Even having won four of the six, I dared not sit down to my prize lest I enter the land of Nod. Crazy Mike laughed, turned on Air Supply's "Winter Wonderland."

"We have two different lifestyles," I sighed. "You're nocturnal and I'm diurnal."

Fast forward twenty years to the Outer, Outer, Outer, Outer Excelsior in the Bedlam Blue Bungalow. Aidan has a sleep disorder, which turns out to be a competitive advantage. Many mornings, as I walk out the door at five, I'll notice that during the wee hours, Aidan has converted the Lego Deathstar into a Jacob's ladder. When I shrugged, "Normal children do not perform science experiments in the middle of the night" he shrugged right back to say, "Really? You're lecturing me about normal?"

Diane Scottini, a Chronicle reader, wrote, "Having a teenager means going to bed and praying for daylight."

The night before Aidan's first high school interview, we had one of those frenzied Fridays that ended with cops at two am. Now, I didn't even interview for college, and that was Notre Dame. I didn't even interview for graduate school. But nowadays 13- and 14-year-olds have to put on tuxedos, and convince a panel they will reinvent string theory.

6:29 am: I dragged myself out of bed, threw myself out of the shower to find Aidan dressed in a white shirt, blue khakis, and a blue pullover, fresh and ready to go. He explained, "I just never went to bed. This way I'm not tired."

"Wear one of my ties," I advised on the supposition that no one in Frank wears a tie anymore, so it would give him a leg up. I picked out a green one that Uncle Jon had given me the last time I went looking for a job, so it was an antique.

We got to the school (I'm not naming it in case we don't get in), and this nice woman took him away for an interview. When she returned, she asked, "Who coached this young man?"

Brian looked at me. I looked at Brian. "Well, I did pick out the tie, but other than that he was on his own."

She smiled, "Well, the tie was pretty retro, but I don't think I have ever met another eighth grader to be this self-aware. He told me how much he hates math, but that hummingbirds are the only creatures who can fly backwards. He's going to be interesting at whatever school he ends up in."

Crazy Mike always likes it when there's a moral to the story so here it is: sometimes growing up in chaos is good. It teaches you to have a Plan B.

The Roadmap of Where We Have Been

THIS IS a column I did not want to write. When I got to work on Monday morning, my boss noticed that I had a scrape on that little stretch of skin between the thumb and the index finger. It's one of those places where a band-aid will not stay.

In April I'm leading a workshop, and one of my first writing prompts is: "Tell me the story of your tattoo." There are 45 million people in the United States with at least one tattoo, which means that there are at least 45 million stories. Twenty percent of all American adults have what Mordecai calls a tramp stamp, and it's likely the percentage is much higher for adults living in California. The census bureau doesn't keep this statistic, but unofficial sources put San Francisco as the seventh most tattooed city in the United States.

For the record, I have two. When I got the first, back in Ann Arbor, this self-described "tough old biker broad" etched a star into my ankle telling me that when I get old, and someone sasses me, I can drop my pants and say, 'See? You're not the only one who's ever been young and stupid!'"

Now not everyone likes their tattoo. My roommate from police academy, Brian, got a mermaid when he was in the Coast Guard, only when the Starbucks logo came out, it looked exactly like his left forearm, so he paid a couple thousand to get it removed. To this day he won't drink a latte.

Back to the class: there's always a student who grumbles, "But I don't have a tattoo."

I reply, "Then tell me about the one you would have."

If the person says, "I can't make up a story like that," I shrug, "If you can't make up a story, maybe a writing class isn't the best way to spend your money."

But for the determined I say, "Tell me the story of your scar. And before anyone asks, we all have scars."

There's one on my thigh from the day I learned how not to ride motorcycles. There's a faded one on my forehead from the homophobic defensive tactics instructor.

Aidan's got one on his arm from the incision. Zane's got one on his eyebrow from a run-in with a door hinge in the seventh grade. The square of fur on Buddyboy's back, from his ACL surgery, has still not grown in five months later.

The Bedlam Blue Bungalow in the Outer, Outer, Outer, Outer Excelsior has scars on its kitchen cabinets. The sofas. The stained glass windows.

We all have scars. They are the roadmap of where we have been.

Zane came back in December. We saw a lot of psychiatrists, psychologists and social workers. We sat in therapy where we each had to draw the family as animals. For the record, all four drew me as a dog. But I drew Brian as a unicorn.

We tried to be supportive fathers, Fred MacMurray and Sheriff Andy Taylor. We registered him for school. We taught him how to boil spaghetti.

But Zane was not quite ready to come home. Not yet. He made a lot of wrong choices, and since no Fisher-Paulson ever does anything small, these choices were a disaster. And for once, Aidan got to be the hero of the tale.

This is not the tragic ending. This is the semi-tragic middle.

We're still gonna tell the story of this family because we are not unique. Sarah and Jill have sent a child away so the child could come back better. Even Crazy Mike. We had to figure with the Fisher-Paulsons it would take two tries. Every family has a place where it was torn open, but that scar also means that the wound has healed. Rumi said that scars are "the place where the Light enters you."

Almost two years ago, I asked you readers to light a candle, to whisper, "I do believe in Fisher-Paulsons." So don't stop believing now. Have faith that one day we all will be home together.

Mark Hett, one of my readers, wrote, "You are in my atheist prayers." And we can't ask for anything better than that: that the story of this wayward family inspires even the most faithless to trust in something. Atheist prayers count twice.

That little scrape at my metacarpaphalangeal joint will one day be a scar. And that scar will be a story. Let's make it one of hope.

Never Retreat

SISTER LIL (her rap name is Lil Sistah) gave me a homework as-signment, which I resented because even though I'm close to fin-ishing the 56th grade, I already do all of Aidan's Algebra and History.

But this was the week of the eighth-grade retreat, where the students who have spent almost a decade at Saint John the Evange-list prepared for high school. "We have asked each of the parents to write a letter," she said, "because this is a rite of passage, when they stop being boys and girls and they start being young men and young women."

Sister Shirley had already given me the homework of chaperon-ing the cherubs on this retreat, so I asked my husband Brian if he would write the note and he replied, "Sister Lil didn't ask for cho-reography. After thirty-five years, you need to remember: I'm the dancer. You're the writer."

So, I wrote:

February 2020

Dear Aidan:

In the winter of 1976, when I was just about your age, Hap and Nurse Vivian sent me on a retreat with the Marist Brothers in Eso-pus, a tiny village in upstate New York. I had never much been out-side of Ozone Park at the time. My dad sent me a letter to be read that weekend. He wrote, "Even though you're a nerd, you're gifted with a fine sense of humor. You'll never make the headlines, but you will do good things."

My relationship with Hap was awkward: straight dad/gay son. But we both had a love of words. He was a poet, but more often he was a father.

And because of him, at that retreat I decided what I wanted to be when I grew up: a writer. Since then, I've had a lot of different jobs: waiter, cook, sales manager, buyer, marketing director, deputy sheriff, but that weekend I learned that I would always turn to prose.

Likely you think your relationship with me is just as awkward as mine was with Hap: gay dad/straight son.

And then there's Zane. For fourteen years, you've lived with the Kim Kardashian of older brothers, famous for nothing other than being infamous. While you struggled with the multiplication table, he failed out altogether, so you were on your own more than the average.

What is a father's legacy? When Hap died, the funeral director said that it was the loudest wake he'd ever been to: Brothers X, XX, and I told stories because that is what Hap would have done. A part of me will always be Hap (and a part of me Nurse Vivian) and let me admit to you now that all of my Dad jokes were his jokes.

One day you may find that part of you will come from Papa, and part of you (the funny part) will come from me.

Here are the lessons I've tried to teach:

1. Most days love is complicated and doesn't make sense.
2. The secret to making a good chili is to grate the cinnamon stick directly into the pot.
3. You don't have to be a normal family to be good or to have fun. You just have to be a family.
4. None of us know where we are going, or what we are doing.
5. Just because you're mad doesn't mean you get to be mean.
6. Be kind.

And about morals? Sister Lil told me that I've already taught you what you need to know. It's up to you whether to do it.

But you have also taught me:

1. A hummingbird is the only creature who can fly backwards.
2. Having challenges doesn't mean you love any less. It just means that the love is different.
3. When you follow your heart, like a wolf follows the moon, you will never truly go wrong.
4. Having fun together is a big part of being family. Thank you for the jigsaw puzzles.
5. Sometimes donuts for dinner does make sense.

Hap was right. I never did make the headlines, but I am "above the fold" in the best newspaper in the world.

A father always wants his son's life to be better than his own. I don't know if you will have any epiphanies this weekend. I hope that when you leave the Outer, Outer, Outer, Outer Excelsior, that you will reach everything you dream for, and I hope you dream big. But in the meantime, you will do good things.

And all of your Dad jokes will be mine.

Love,

Dad

Dandelions on Pizza

THE DAYS are getting longer, sunset arriving an hour later with the clocks sprung forward. This week the California lilacs in the Outer, Outer, Outer, Outer Excelsior have burst purple, with fat bees hovering around the Bedlam Blue Bungalow. In our backyard the calla lilies grow their white petals despite the lack of February rain. Down the block, the Roof Cow has donned her kilt and wears a sign: "Kiss me. I'm corned beef."

Spring has sprung. My husband Brian and I have already bought tomato plants to kill off. And while other men's thoughts are turning to baseball, mine turn towards bread.

Nurse Vivian baked soda bread this time of year for Saint Patrick's Day. It's not an ancient Celtic tradition, really dating back only to 1843, when pearl ash, or potash, was first brought to the Emerald Isle. It mixed well with the soft wheat (low gluten) grown there and when buttermilk was added, it bubbled up. Simple recipe, really not needing more than four ingredients. In the north, it's quartered and turned into farl, but Nurse Vivian's family, the Kinirys, came from Cork. The recipe was on a penny postcard, including the instruction to "cut a cross in the dough to let the devil out."

"Why do you put caraway seeds in?" I once asked.

Nurse Vivian rolled the raisins into the dough, "It keeps a husband from wandering."

My parents moved to South Ozone Park in the spring of 1953. Just north of then-Idlewild Airport, the neighborhood was a blend of nations. East of 131st Street were the Latino families. North of Rockaway Boulevard there were the Polish and Jewish families, where Hi and Esther's Soda Shop sold egg creams. The streets surrounding Saint Anthony of Padua Church were mainly Italian, except for Sutter Avenue, which was the one Irish block. We lived on Sutter Avenue.

Which made our next door neighbors, the Carbones, unique. Louis Carbone was married to Margaret Maguire, an Irish woman in an Italian marriage living on the Irish block of the Italian parish. Margie translated the Sicilian to the Gaelic, like why Stallone's Bakery put dandelions on the pizza in March: "Segni di Primavera; Signs of Spring."

But mixed neighborhoods weren't anything new. In fact, Saint Patrick was born in Roman Britain then emigrated to Eire. Apparently, Hadrian hadn't finished his wall yet.

Nurse Vivian told me that one of the first Sundays that the Paulsons attended Saint Anthony's, when the mass ended, the nuns served everyone bread. She thought it was in honor of Saint Patrick, but Margie explained, "La Tavala de San Giuseppe."

My mother liked the idea of the Table of Saint Joseph, the foster father of Jesus, but asked, "They don't put caraway in the bread?"

"They put in sesame, for the tears of Saint Joseph." It wasn't until I became a foster father that I knew why Joseph cried so much.

23andme insists that I am 72.0% Irish, Aidan 26.1%, Brian 18.3% and even Zane sneaking in with 4.2%. But really, we are all Irishmen, living in a British / French / African American / Native American / Asian family, on a block where no two houses in a row have the same nationality, in one of the most diverse cities in the nation. There's no such thing as "an Irish parish" or "an Italian Parish" in San Francisco, though they do call Most Holy Redeemer "the gays and the grays."

But there's a little Nurse Vivian in me. This week, we're all Irish for the most American of Irish traditions. Aidan pinches anyone who doesn't wear green which is problematic only in the fact that he's color blind.

We bake my mother's soda bread. We still cut a cross, though Aidan cuts a Star of David in one of the loaves for our Jewish relatives. I still put in caraway seeds, and it works. Thirty-five years with Brian and he hasn't wandered away yet.

In California, the only creatures who celebrate Saint Joseph's Day, however, are the swallows returning to Capistrano. But on that day, I remember Nurse Vivian's story of the Irish woman in the Italian marriage.

Margie Maguire Carbone still lives in South Ozone Park. She reads my column, and never fails to tell me when I use too much blarney. She taught us that it didn't matter semolina or soda or sourdough. It only matters that we break bread together, and we tell stories, like why they put the dandelions on the pizza.

Love in the Time of Corona

AIDAN caught the sniffles at his retreat. He lounged on the La-Z-Boy, and though able to operate the television remote, he was too sick to study Algebra.

"Do you think I'm dying of Covid?" he asked. And all at once, a tiny little acronym, short for COronaVIrus Disease of 2019, had reached the Outer, Outer, Outer, Outer Excelsior.

"You're not dying. You've had a stuffy nose since the day we adopted you. Truly, you look up the word 'grippe' in Webster's Dictionary, and you will find the name Aidan Fisher-Paulson."

Other parents would have had a Hallmark moment. Nurse Vivian would make sweet warm tea with cinnamon toast, but cinnamon is too spicy for my son, so instead he drank ginger ale with hot Cheetos. I'm in the high-risk group so you'd think I'd avoid Typhoid Aidan, but he's a teenager. He naturally avoids me.

Long-term readers know we're related to Calamity Jane Canary, and though we've dropped the Canary/Kiniry, we retain the Calamity.

This is the second plague I've lived through. Well, at least so far. I was in the high-risk group then, as well, though there was a lot more shame. Or rather shaming.

Summer of 1981 at the University of Michigan in Ann Arbor, I led a "coming out" group with the Pink Triangle Collective. On the week that we talked about health, my co-facilitator, Danny, pulled out a New York Times clipping about a "Rare Cancer Seen in Homosexuals."

The irony had not been lost on me that I'd come out on the exact wrong day. There were more articles about Acquired Immunodeficiency Disorder (AIDS), notably by San Francisco Chronicle reporter Randy Shilts.

And then it got real. By the time that I moved back to New York, the end times had begun. David Norrie was my first friend to die, and then a funeral every week.

We got angry, because the government wasn't doing enough to keep us safe. We formed the first national AIDS switchboard, to dispel the rumors. We didn't know whom to love, whom to touch, but we knew enough to tell people that they wouldn't get it from their Haitian cotton couch.

We formed the AIDS Coalition to Unleash Power, ACTUP.

Thirty-two million people have died from the Human Immunodeficiency Virus (HIV), including Zane's first uncle, Tim. I'm a light-one-candle-rather-than-curse-the-darkness kind of guy, and if you are as well, then support the Terry Asten Bennett, the woman who runs Cliff's Variety. She's the bus mom for the AIDS Life Cycle, and she's trying to raise money to fight that scourge.

Fast forward to the scourge *du jour*. I'm in a different place than I was in 1981, decades past the age where I worry about the exchange of body fluids.

But there are a few lessons from then that we can use now. The big one is not to blame anybody for a virus. Not the gays, not the Chinese, not the Italians. We don't need scapegoats. We need compassion. We need to be kind.

There are a few parallels. It's likely that Corona beer won't do much better than the Ayds Candy line.

It seems like everyone is home sheltering in place, but the downside to being a deputy is that I don't get to call in sick for

Armageddon. We cannot telecommute emergency service, so we show up. I've been working 12-hour days, seven days a week, since the mayor declared an emergency.

But Aidan got at least two weeks off from school, thanks to the generosity of the archdiocese. Which means that he has Papa as his full-time teacher, and if Aidan thought Sister Lil was tough, he's got Professor Snape now.

The new schoolhouse is the Bedlam Blue Bungalow, and everything is a teachable moment when you're homeschooling. Even the pandemic. Given his unique challenges, we haven't had to teach him about social distance. We taught him emotional proximity was more important.

We tell Aidan to cover his sneezes. We tell him to keep his fingers (and toes) out of his mouth.

"Stay informed," I say.

To which he replies, "Did you know it's named for the crown-like spikes on its surface?"

To which Papa replies, "Not the tiara I was hoping for."

"We can each of us die at any moment, Aidan, but what's important is how we live. In the meantime, we wash our hands. We've been told that other families sing 'Happy Birthday' to get the full twenty seconds, but the Fisher-Paulsons sing, *'I Will Survive'*."

Extreme Parenting

OPENED UP the Chronicle last week, and couldn't find my column on its usual back page. In fact, couldn't find Datebook at first, but then my husband Brian held up another section and said, "Now you know it's the end times. Kevin Fisher-Paulson is on the Sports Page."

Brother X and Brother XX read the electronic version of the Voice of the West, so they will not know this. Otherwise, they'd be writing to the editor about how my only athletic accomplishment was a trophy engraved in 1970 as follows: League's Worst Bowler.

Still these are strange days, and with most arenas closed the Chronicle is covering the sport called "Extreme Parenting." The only stadium open is the Bedlam Blue Bungalow in the Outer, Outer, Outer, Outer Excelsior and the score so far: 40 Love, but sometimes 40 Hate. Zane is back again. This is probably the only good we will see out of the pandemic.

Aidan hates Papa more than me because Papa is stuck at home with social distance learning. By the time I get home these days, his ADHD medication has worn off. I did try to teach him geometry the other day, but he went off on a tangent.

But Aidan does save up some of the good venom for me. When he wants me to buy an app he tells me that I'm very brave for working with the police, firefighters and nurses to keep the city safe. When I decline the offer to purchase "Mafia Zombie Killers 5" he says, "You do know you're the worst father in the world. You probably have that virus in your pocket right now."

Aidan's not quite a germaphobe, but he has thrown all of the Corona beer out of the house.

And there's a little bit of me that feels guilty that he might be right, that I might bring something home. While the city shelters in place, we've been guarding the hospital, and the quarantine sites, and just about any other place you could pick up a germ.

Deputy Sheriffs are a bit strange. I've known them to do extraordinarily brave things these past few weeks: confront a man waving a hatchet, give CPR to an unsheltered man with a substance abuse issue. But at the same time, they find things funny that just aren't funny. Like the fact that I'm so old. When we realized that technically I'm in the high-risk group, we joked about the funeral, and whether we would have dancing girls or dancing boys.

"Whatever," I replied, "I won't be around to appreciate either. But make sure I get a bagpiper. You can't have a cop funeral without a bagpiper playing "Amazing Grace." It's like a soda bread without caraway seeds."

The Sheriff's Department doesn't have its own piper, and it costs at least two hundred bucks to get one.

One ambitious Irish captain said, "If it means there's an open chief's job, I'll pay for the bagpipes."

More than a hundred years ago, the Irish came to America after the British had outlawed the practice of their native language and had forbidden them from attending school. Thus, many Irish were illiterate, and when they came to the new world, there not being many farms in Manhattan, they took jobs that didn't require reading. Yes, the police. That's why they call them Paddy Wagons, because the Irish, or Paddys, drove them. Further tangent: a paddywhack refers to an Irishman who likes to drink and brawl, which, if you ask me, is redundant.

Law enforcement being a dangerous profession (a police officer is killed in the line of duty every 58 hours), the paddys liked to have the memory of home at their funeral, that being the bagpipes, playing a song written by a sailor named John Newton, who nearly drowned off the Irish coast.

Back to the Outer, Outer, Outer, Outer Excelsior. Brian cooked chicken stew with biscuits. After we toasted the best boys in the world, Zane asked me, "How was your day?" I tried to tell the story. Only it wasn't funny. Not to regular people. Zane started crying and I said, "I have no intention of dying."

"That's just the thing, Dad. You have no intention, but you can't promise."

"Zane, I took an oath to do this job, even when it's dangerous. I'm pretty tough, but none of us know when it's our turn to hear the bagpipes."

Months ago, when Zane went away, we lit a candle, which sat by the window, to light his way safely home. So that night, Zane lit the candle, so I'd know the way home.

I cannot wait to get back to abnormal.

Communion Pringles

NURSE VIVIAN and Hap used to take us out to Yaphank for summer vacations. At that time, eastern Long Island was truly
rural, and so on Sunday, the only service was conducted by a priest
at the firehouse. Nurse Vivian called this "our temporary tradition."
It wasn't bad really and as an added benefit, every once in a while, the
sirens would go off in the middle of Father Hugo's sermon.

Kindness matters. And repetition. It's the little rituals we practice that keep us going, that remind us of what does not change.

We're living in makeshift times. We can't shake hands so we
bump elbows. We can't go to the barber, so we buy a set of clippers.

Crazy Mike canceled his trip to Hawaii on Day Two of the Pandemic, but has been wearing a face mask with pineapples to remind
him that after all this, there are warm days on the beach. It's a surprise
to no one that I'm wearing a Batman mask, and for Marvel days I
have a Spider-man one.

I gave up coffee for Lent last year and never got back to it. But
I've worked 36 out of the past 38 days, twelve-to-fourteen hour shifts,
and about a week ago, I got to work, and thought, "I can't do it. I
just don't have the stamina to put on these boots, this vest and this
belt." It must have shown on my face because Crazy Mike showed up
two minutes later with a chai tea latte in his hand, sighing, "There are
times when it's good to have a vice or two."

He's shown up every morning since, with just enough caffeine to
get me through Armageddon.

These are the little kindnesses. Crazy Mike knows how to read me. He keeps a baggie of crackers in his desk, and on those days when the sky is falling, and we've got to find shelter for thirty unsheltered people, and people are looking at me to figure out how to do it, Crazy Mike reaches into his desk, and asks, "Would a Triscuit help?" Sonavagun it always does.

Most days I don't talk politics or religion with my fellow deputies. There's this one guy, let's call him M, who I like, but given the Reagan memorabilia in his office, I've known enough to keep my mouth shut. Even so, we were talking about what we missed in the normal world, and I told him that Brian and I missed Sundays at Most Holy Redeemer. M replied that he was Catholic too. Long Distance Transubstantiation: his family watched the mass on television together, and to go along with their grape juice, for communion wafers they used Pringles.

My sons Zane and Aidan do not miss Father Matt's sermons, maybe because they are never saved by the fire alarm. This is not a "spirited child" kind of thing. This is a teenager thing. Other than Supermario and Princess Peach, they don't listen to any adult. But we have our own kind of liturgy, and just like the Roman Catholics, we repeat certain phrases, we tell each other stories and we break bread.

At just about dusk, I walk through the door and say, "Daddy's home." And the boys repeat, "Daddy's home!" and everybody gets hugged until Buddyboy wags his tail fast enough for us to remember that dogs need their ears scratched once in a while. Bandit never learned how to operate his tail, but he's the only canine in domesticity to have mastered rolling his eyes and sighing.

Then dinner. We humans sit down, hold hands and say Grace. Zane's hand used to rest in mind, but now, just before the Amen, he flips mine over to let me know that my days as the alpha are numbered. I toast, "The best boys in the world!" to which we all say, "Wherever they are!" We ask each other how our day was and even if it's un-frozen pizza, we're breaking crust together.

This column takes a village. It's not just the Fisher-Paulsons who inhabit the Bedlam Blue Bungalow. It's not just Crazy Mike and Brother X and Brother XX or even the ghosts of Tim and Nurse Vivian. It's all of you, reading every week, expecting the stories to be repeated, expecting that if I write one Outer, there will undoubtedly be three Outers following it before I get to Excelsior. On Wednesday mornings, it's you and us, *fractionis panis in absentia,* a virtual cup of coffee. Have what you like: chai tea, Triscuits or Pringles.

Teen Angels

NURSE VIVIAN always said that of her three sons she "liked the dog best." She didn't start saying this until July 20, 1971, my thirteenth birthday. Less than fifty years later I get it. Whiskers may have been a mutt, but he was infinitely more manageable than Brother X, Brother XX or me.

The Fisher-Paulsons call Stephanie Anne Schrandt Boone by her initials: Sasb. In fact, she has large chrome versions of those letters on her desk. In return, she calls us the Kipcops. She and her husband Mordecai have what is called neurotypical children. The four of them have sheltered in place, taken hikes and played family game night. Gotta admit I was jealous until she texted me, to tell me that after living in the same house for five weeks now, "One of my children took the initials and rearranged them to 'ASSB.'"

"How do you know it wasn't Mordecai?" I asked.

"Because teenagers are jerks," she said. "I honestly don't know how our species has survived with teenagers always being the next generation."

"And yet they think we're the jerks," I commiserated.

Which brings me to the Outer, Outer, Outer, Outer Excelsior. Good news: Zane must be paying attention in math class because he now refers to it as 'Excelsior to the Outer^4'.

I had two days off, and this was Zane's last two days off before returning to Hogwarts. That's right, first part of the pandemic, they sent Zane home. It's not sad anymore, him returning. Well, maybe just a little sad. Sometimes I feel like I'm always saying goodbye to Zane, like I'm his part-time father.

I wanted the perfect weekend, full of cinnamon rolls and horticulture.

We don't garden much but last year, by some miracle Brian had kept three Heirloom Fog tomato plants alive long enough to make a batch of chili. So this year we drove to Sloat's in search of peppers and lettuce. I asked the boys what kind of bean plants they wanted, and Aidan advised, "Jelly." Otherwise, the boys stayed in the car.

When we returned to the Bedlam Blue Bungalow, Zane and Aidan hid in their respective bedrooms while Brian and I played Oliver and Lisa Douglas in the backyard. ("Farm spreading out so far and wide...")

Although the boys ignored us, the dogs were enthusiastic. In fact, both Buddyboy and Bandit insisted on watering the plants over and over.

But all that work on the back nine got us hungry.

Remember when I wrote I'd given up red meat for Lent this year? For Easter, our Fairy Godsister sent us a lamb roast, stew meat, chuck roast, steak, pork chop, rump roast, meatballs, sirloin tip, hot dogs and even knockwurst. A carnivore's tour of San Francisco. So I tossed a random slab of tenderloin into the oven, and while I peeled Yukon Golds and chopped Brussel sprouts I mused that my children were still enchambered.

What had happened to those afternoons of watching superhero movies together, playing Uno at the dining room table? What do they do instead? Aidan hides out in the Brat-cave performing science experiments: What happens if you shove a Pop Tart down the furnace vent? What happens when you put bubble bath down the toilet?

Zane hides out to text a girl who he won't tell me is his girlfriend, but when she pings his iPad, he rushes out of the living room. I won't mention her name, because of her father. The parent of every child who my son dates is a potential in-law.

I'd overcooked this particular beast. It was tough. But the mashed potatoes were perfect at the exact proportion of half tuber/ half butter. We sat and held hands, and this was the victory I got: we weren't together solving a jigsaw puzzle this weekend, but for one hour, we did chew and chew and chew that meat together. And we laughed. Aidan told us how he had defeated Slender Man, and Zane told me about the girl, who he still won't admit is his girlfriend, but who he does admit is "very sweet."

Never expect a clean victory. The other fifty-nine hours they did what teenagers do: avoid their parents. I always worry that these things are straight-adopted-black-special-needs-children/gay-adopted-white-special-needs-parents things. But every human who passes the age of twelve finds that their own bedroom is more interesting than sitting in the living room with their parents watching *Murder She Wrote*.

Take the win.

Papas and the Poppas

B EFORE I met my husband Brian thirty-five years ago, I didn't date a lot of men. There was a harpist, a mafia hitman, and a cowboy named Theodore. And Scott.

Scott was Jewish. Years later I realized that our relationship was based not upon mutual attraction but rather fascination with each other's religion. Scott loved all my Catholic inhibitions and ritual idiosyncrasies ("Let me get this right: you skip meat on Fridays but otherwise you eat as much bacon as you please. The guy leading the service wears a dress and carries a smoking purse.")

Whereas I loved the hamentashen. And the lighting of candles. The Chag Pesach Samech.

I spoke no Hebrew. He spoke no Latin. I dabbled in Yiddish. He dabbled in guilt. Took me a while to figure out that his father wasn't calling me Scott's guy, but rather Scott's goy.

At Christmas time, Scott explained that his family, went out for dim sum at House of Chang. This was their tradition, distinct and separate from the Christians in the Red Hook neighborhood of Brooklyn. "It kept us from getting jealous of the flocked trees and egg nog."

Scott eventually broke up with me because I did not use hair conditioner.

Which brings me to Mother's Day.

Fifteen years ago, gay adoption wasn't *au courant,* and most counties had not yet updated the forms. So, on March 25, 2005, when a judge established that Zane would be our forever son, I looked down at the paperwork and saw that Brian would be his forever father, and I would be his forever… mother.

And yes, Crazy Mike did say, "The rest of us always thought of you as a big mother."

So, although I'm technically the mom, I get no benefit. Come the second Sunday of May, there are no cards, no flowers, no breakfast in bed. Mother's Day is as exotic to the Fisher-Paulsons as Purim or Eidh.

Nurse Vivian passed away on May 8, 2002, and the following Sunday, Mother's Day, I gave her eulogy. Eerie that Nana, Brian's mother, passed away on Mother's Day 2014, and so the holiday for us is more like Orphan's Day. While others are making brunch, we acknowledge that each of Fisher-Paulsons: Brian, our sons Zane and Aidan, our dogs Buddyboy and Bandit, have all been orphans. And have rescued each other.

We've made our own family out of broken parts. It's not the Von Trapp. It's not the Partridges or the Bradys. We're more like the Papas and the Poppas, with me playing Poppa Cass Elliot.

The upside of a pandemic: this is the first year that little orphan Aidan hasn't had to explain to his teacher why he's the only one in the class not drawing a flower on construction paper for Mother's Day cards. So far, they've done no arts and crafts on Zoom.

The boys do send cards to Aunt Dee, Aunt JJ, the Terry Asten Bennett and Sasb, the wonder women in our lives. Even Uncle Doya, who is really Aunt Doya. But a little part of me feels guilty that on Mother's Day Zane and Aidan come up with empty air.

It's with great irony, therefore, that Buddyboy and Bandit became the same-sex parents of an orphan puppy this week.

She's oddly colored, mostly white with a circle of black fur around her right eye, like Petey in the Little Rascals, or a Lucky Strike smoker. She's mostly Pekingese, though I suspect she has a little coyote in her. Another orphan has rescued us.

Naming has its own magic. Each of us took on a different name when we became a Fisher-Paulson. I was a Paulson. Brian was a Fisher. We invented Zane and Aidan. Buddyboy was a compromise, in that I wanted to call him Buddy, and Zane wanted to call him Boy. And Bandit stole our hearts.

So, the hour we carried her into the Bedlam Blue Bungalow in the Outer, Outer, Outer, Outer Excelsior, she looked and sounded and swashbuckled like a buccaneer puppy, not Queen Anne's Vengeance, but the Pirate Queen.

For others, the baby boom will be in nine months, after all the sheltering in place. But for us it's now, and it's a puppy boom. There's something very hopeful about a puppy. No saving up for college or braces. Just four paws skidding across the wooden floor and learning how to wag her tail. She makes for a most unusual Mother's Day. It keeps us from getting jealous of the flocked trees and egg nog.

Welcome to the family, Queenie. May we all live happily ever after.

The Color Purple

WHEN YOU READ this column, likely you see it in black and white. But for me it's the color purple.

The Sheriff's Department hired a new safety analyst a few months back, and when the time came for him to order stationery supplies he asked for a purple pen. "We don't do that," the Sergeant (Crazy Mike) replied, "You can order blue or black, but *he's* the only one who writes with a lavender quill."

The "he" that Crazy Mike was referring to is me. It started with marksmanship. When I went out to the range, I had to sign in. On top of the roster was a magenta Ener-gel. Now I hated shooting, but I loved the writing. On his last day, the Range Master handed it to me saying, "Cops will always steal a blue pen if you leave it there. But they leave this one alone."

It became my quirk. Well, one of my quirks. Like the Captain America shield in my office. Or the fact that I schedule meetings for times like 0948 hours.

Crazy Mike puts up with my eccentricities, and I put up with Crazy Mike putting up with my eccentricities. I do not point out to him that his taking pictures of abandoned shoes is a little odd. I do not suggest that buying his wife a crematorium niche for Christmas is unconventional.

Back to the purple pen. It's not just a gay thing, though other deputies see it as such. Partly it's that I do like to hold onto my writing device, and the Range Master was right: straight deputies tend not to steal boysenberry ballpoints. Part of it is because it makes it a lot easier for me to pick out my name on a list. I'm the one with the mauve moniker.

But it also lets people know that I am different, and I'm okay with being different. You either laugh at me or with me.

Besides, purple's got a history. Purple didn't show up much in nature. As civilizations developed, so did fabric, and dyes. Blues and greens and yellows. But it took until about 1900 BC before this Phoenician figured out that if you crushed some twelve thousand murex shellfish you got a gram and a half of purple dye. This is why it was the color of emperors and royalty. In fact, Julius Caesar proclaimed that only he could wear that color.

Nowadays, it's still rare. For example, other than the rainbow flag, there are very few countries that use plum on their pennants. I can think of Dominica and the Balearic Islands but leave any others to my very clever readership.

Do you know why night scopes are in green? Because our eyes have the easiest time discriminating between shades of green, but the hardest time discriminating heliotrope.

But me, it's what I do. And it's not just any pen. The one thing Crazy Mike and I agree on is that fountain pens won't do. For him, it's because he's left-handed. For me, it's because I tend to nibble on the end of them, and the last thing I want is a mouthful of magenta. When I teach writing classes, I tell my students that it doesn't matter what paper you write on, but you must write with a pen you love: the weight of the barrel, the smell of the grape ink, the way it flows across the page. I may leave the Glock 19 and the handcuffs at work but I always carry my lilac plume. All week long I jot notes with it into a spiral notebook. And I do it in cursive, because my sons still cannot read that.

Every column has a critical mass, a moment in which it must be written. Might be on a foggy Sunday morning. Might be thirteen minutes before deadline. But the purple prose has never failed me. Those notes tumble together and become what you are reading right now. It's not Proust. It's not even Herb Caen. But it will do. I haven't figured out why, and I'm not supposed to. It's like a bicycle. Or God. If I think too much about how it works then it doesn't work anymore.

What's all this got to do with the Outer, Outer, Outer, Outer Excelsior? For one, Zane and Aidan know that they don't have to write that essay on Alice Walker with a Bic ballpoint. They can use a green pencil, black charcoal, heck, even a turquoise crayon. For us in the Bedlam Blue Bungalow, nothing is just plain black-and-white.

For us, it's fifty shades of violet.

Banana Bread

Because Hap (my Dad) worked at what used to be Idlewild, but then became JFK airport, he always got deals on stuff that had "fallen off the plane" and so we had exotic foods like pineapples and bananas. This meant Nurse Vivian baked banana bread "in case a neighbor dropped by." The recipe was a stepchild of her soda bread, leaving out the buttermilk, and putting in the sweet plantains and vanilla instead. Simple, no fussing around with nutmeg and cloves, and, as only Nurse Vivian could do, she made it in a blender.

On Tuesday, November 9, 1965, at 5:27 pm, the Eastern seaboard lost all power. Hap liked to have dinner at 5:30 and this would have been a disaster, but Nurse Vivian lit a candle, got out the kerosene lamps and transistor radios, and we had a picnic on the stoop, the Carbones on our right, the McCaffreys on our left.

There was a full moon, and Frank Cadden broke out the beer. He also set up a barbecue so we could grill the pork chops and hamburgers that were thawing because the freezers were out. Brothers X and XX organized stickball by flashlight, while Lisa Mangels beat me in a game of hopscotch.

A few Rheingolds into it, Jeannie McCormick sang old Maguire Sisters songs, followed by my mother reciting "The Face on the Barroom Floor." Sadie Cadden asked Nurse Vivian, "What do you think it is? The Russians invading?"

Joey McCaffery, who taught me how to be a nerd, suggested, "Maybe the electromagnetic field of a UFO?"

Nurse Vivian handed them both a slice of banana bread. "Whatever it is, we're together."

We could have sat on the stoop any night, but the disaster made for the only evening in Queens when we could see the stars.

Nowadays, the Fisher-Paulsons don't get cozy catastrophes: we get the no-sleep-at-three-in-the-morning-emergency-broken-arm-colostomy-ruptured-disc kind, not the kind we can share with the neighbors.

So, I'm gonna sound crazy, and I know we're not over this yet, but there are parts of this quarantine that I am enjoying. No traffic. The freedom to cut my hair with clippers. The "Outer, Outer, Outer, Outer Excelsior Strong!"

Something about a tragedy reminds us to be kind.

It started with my husband Brian. The 43 bus hasn't been running, and a few of our neighbors are elderly (which means older than me), so Brian picked up extra groceries at Safeway. One Friday he returned with 25 onions, and I asked, "Okay, I get the good neighbors part, but do any of them eat two dozen Vidalias at a time?"

Brian shrugged, and sliced. And cried. Four hours later, he had a quart of French Onion Soup for Christina, and Aunt JJ and Aunt Helene, and Aunt Dorla, and even a vegan quart for Maya, the girl next door. Matching croutons for each.

Next day Aunt JJ and Aunt Helene sent back the bowls we had dropped off but had filled them with lemon bars.

We Fisher-Paulsons are competitive. If they were going to be kind, then we were going to be even kinder. Saturday morning, we chopped potatoes, carrots and rosemary and rolled out crust and we delivered chicken pot pies, in individual tins, to the Outer Excelsiorites.

Including Susan, the Roof Cow's Mother. Yes, Virginia, there is a Roof Cow. I guarantee you that if you address a letter to Susan, the

House with a Cow on Top, San Francisco, it will get to her. The next day, Susan rang the doorbell, having filled those tins with donuts topped with a raspberry glaze so sweet you could taste the rasp.

And Aidan, on his fifteenth birthday, walked around the neighborhood delivering slices of wolf cake, earning him enough service credits to get that virtual graduation on the 6th. Yes, for those of you who worried, Sister Lil summoned up the prayers of the entire Ursuline order and transubstantiated that F in English into a D minus.

Tiffany, a mother of one of Aidan's schoolmates, made paella, and we sat on dining room chairs six feet apart on her lawn and told stories until the wind blew cool down the San Bruno Mountains with that first hint of the fog that makes this town so splendid, and the boys lit sparklers. Likely I'd have recited "The Face on the Barroom Floor" if I knew all the verses.

This is the new world order. Instead of banana bread, we make raspberry donuts. And still, "Whatever it is, we're together."

LGBTQQIA2

IN A NORMAL YEAR, this week's column would have been my "50 years of Gay Pride." 51 in Greenwich Village Standard Time, 50 in the Castro, a year behind but always better, although there's an argument that we got the whole thing rolling a year earlier in Compton.

I'm not saying there's no pride this year, it's just virtual, but, pride, let alone gayness, is a hard thing to social distance.

Fifty years ago, it was gay pride, as gay was then an umbrella term. Quite rightly we began to recognize the full spectrum of the rainbow, and evolved into something like: LGBTQQIA2: Lesbian, Gay, Bisexual, Transgender, Queer, Questioning, Intersex, Asexual, Two-Spirited. Notice the Q's: Queer and Questioning, but not Queen.

The term queer was first used in the trial of Oscar Wilde, when the Marquis of Queensbury called him a "snob queer." Wilde ended up in Reading Jail and died an early death, but the pejorative long outlived him.

Back in Ozone Park I had no idea what I was, but when Uncle Eddie said about one of our in-laws: "He's queer as a three-dollar bill" Nurse Vivian gasped and I thought, "Maybe I better stop at two-dollar bill."

I was in the building the night in lower Manhattan when Queer Nation reclaimed the sobriquet, but queer never tripped easily across my tongue. Who made the rules about which insults we reclaim?

I referred to my husband Brian and me as "queens" once in a column, and got a harsh e-mail from a gay man, but here's the thing:

queen has history and nobility. It dates back to Dante's "Il Purgatoria." Freddie Mercury was certainly aware of the connotation when he named his band.

For me it means a guy can be comfortable with his feminine side. I was born in Queens. Lived on Queens Boulevard no less. Nurse Vivian's favorite game show was Queen for a Day. In the writing business we call this foreshadowing.

We even named the dog Queenie, her domain, the Outer, Outer, Outer, Outer Excelsior, and her court limited to Buddyboy and Bandit, but a doyenne works with what she's got.

She's not the first royal dog in San Francisco. Back in the 1860's it was alleged that Bummer and Lazarus were the Emperor Norton's hounds. The truth is they were no one's dogs, other than each other's.

Joshua Abraham Norton, having lost his money in a Peruvian rice deal, proclaimed himself "Norton I, Emperor of the United States and Protector of Mexico" in 1859. Now there's a job for you. He ate for free, issued his own money and even decreed that a bridge be built to connect San Francisco to Oakland. He proclaimed that anyone who used the term "Frisco" must pay a $25 fine.

Edward Jump drew a cartoon of Norton with Bummer and Lazarus, but really this Newfoundland and this mutt were famous on their own, legendary for the rescue of runaway horses and the capture of 85 rats in 20 minutes. Mark Twain even wrote Bummer's eulogy.

So, if a guy calls himself an emperor, he gets a suspension bridge built, but if he calls himself a queen, he gets hate mail.

In 1965, Jose Sarria declared herself "the Widow Norton" and founded the Imperial Court System, a charitable organization, which branched out from San Francisco, and to this day, it's the second largest LGBTQQIA2 organization in the world, full of czarinas, sultanas and queens.

Neither Zane nor Aidan are likely to proclaim themselves emperor, and they're equally unlikely to claim any of the acronyms in LGBTQQIA2. Aidan, frankly, is relieved that he doesn't have to march across Market Street this Sunday. He's the kind of teenager who'd rather phone in his protests.

Stay in this weekend. Be as queer as you want. Or as straight. Take a moment to be kind. Call yourself emperor, queen, king or court jester. Make this weekend LGBTQQQIA2-Ynot.

One of the other adoptive parents we know has a child who back in the day, would have been called, "pre-gay." He wears pink ombre. It's still hard. According to Global Citizen, one out of five hate crimes in the United States was committed because of sexual orientation. About 40% of homeless youths identify as LGBTQ. 41% of Transgender persons have attempted suicide, 10-20% of LGB adults as well compared with the rest of the population at 4%.

But this boy and Aidan still play Roblox together. Have I mentioned that Aidan is color blind? So, when he looks at the rainbow flag, he sees shades of gray. Maybe that's not so bad.

(Many thanks to Susan, of the Imperial Order of the Garter, for her tales of the Court.)

Column in My Pocket

I N SUMMER 1985, I went out with Jim Gibbey, one of the last guys I dated before I met Brian. He was from the South, so he fried chicken and spoke in a drawl when convenient. Most of our dates were local, in Brooklyn, on the F line, with occasional trips to Fire Island. I didn't think the relationship was going anywhere but for my birthday, he got tickets for *Sunday in the Park with George,* starring Mandy Patinkin and Bernadette Peters.

We walked to the Booth Theater, getting to our balcony seats just in time to hear the announcement, "Ms. Peters will not be performing in tonight's show..."

"Ah'm gone," he whispered and we climbed over patrons in red velvet seats. He went to the box office and got us tickets for a week later. "Stand-ins are okay. But when Ah want the real thing, nothin' else'll do."

We returned a week later, and Bernadette Peters was indeed brilliant. (Today's coincidence: when she was still Bernadette Lazzara, she was in the same grade as Brother XX back in Saint Anthony of Padua in Ozone Park.)

But this turned out to be our last date. Nowdays it would be called ghosting, but Jim never explained so I can only conclude that I was not the real thing.

Ironically, Brian was performing right down the block in *La Cage Aux Folles* that night.

Crazy Mike insists that I should have "one in the can" for the week that the apocalypse comes and I'm about to miss my deadline. Trouble is that it's our fifteenth week in a row of Armageddon and as yet I haven't missed a cutoff. I'm not the Cal Ripken of journalism, but I'm consistent. Herb Caen famously wrote 14,133,000 words for the Chronicle over 58 years. My husband Brian has lesser aspirations for me, in that he sees me as the Hedda Hopper of the San Francisco Chronicle. One of my readers, Brad Witherspoon, called me the gay Erma Bombeck.

But this column doesn't have a category: Unlike Herb, I don't know the city's glitterati. Unlike Hedda, I don't know anyone famous enough to gossip about. And unlike Erma, our family tilts more towards melodrama than light comedy.

This family, my husband Brian, my sons Zane and Aidan, the dogs Buddyboy, Bandit and Queenie make for an odd set of mismatched parts, less of a china set and more of a quilt. We don't follow a schedule. We couldn't write about Aidan's graduation, for example, because two days before he still owed 197 math problems, and his graduation was in doubt.

And yet, I don't skip deadlines. But there's something about having a column in my pocket that feels like cheating, like summer reruns. This column works without a net. The readers deserve our fresh disasters, not the school we got expelled from two years ago or the sump pump failing last winter.

So it's odd as we stagger through the pandemic that something as mundane as a glamping trip with the Sasbs should throw off my rhythm.

Yes, when the ink is dry on these words, the Fisher-Paulsons will not be in the Outer, Outer, Outer, Outer Excelsior but rather some random town in central California. I honestly don't know where. Sasb just put her finger on a map and said, "We'll rent a house here."

Just the two families isolating together rather than separately, less of a mini-vacation and more like a mini-quarantine-come-as-you-are party. Jigsaw puzzles and Pinot Grigio, but no higher ambition.

We haven't gone anywhere since late February, so even crossing the Bay Bridge feels like an adventure.

Why are we going? Truth is, I'm a little jealous that my husband spent the pandemic home with the boys. While I organized patrols, Brian cooked, Aidan learned how to speak sarcasm and Zane got all grown up.

We go away because Aidan has spent the plague in the Bratcave, sulkily coming out once every two hours to put Queenie on the lawn. Somewhere along the line, snacky dinner became snarky dinner.

Crazy Mike's son, Somewhat-Sane Trevor, will be guarding the spoiled hounds, and maybe the time away from puppy Queenie will give my shoelaces time to grow back.

We go away so that we can miss San Francisco again. I love this city in the summer. When Karlotta the Fog comes courting Frank the city, we shiver and put on sweaters, and just a few days away reminds me of how cozy this town is.

And that reminds me of the charm of the Bedlam Blue Bungalow. And that's because of family.

When you want the real thing, nothing else will do.

Lives Matter

THIS IS NOT the funny column. It's the one about race. By the time this gets in print, the protests may be over, but the conflict remains.

Every 39 hours a black person is killed by a peace officer. Black lives matter.

Every 54 hours a peace officer is killed in the line of duty. Blue lives matter.

This is not an equivalence. Every one of these deaths is a tragedy.

Now here's the odd thing: I got into law enforcement because I used to be an activist. I saw how some cops treated minorities and I wanted to do my part to put the peace back into peace officer.

In 1911, Nels Dickmann Anderson published a poem called "The Thin Blue Line" and it came to symbolize that the police in their blue uniforms stood as the border between order and chaos. I do not wear this thin blue line symbol, but then neither do I wear a rainbow flag.

I do wear a badge, because Star #1213 means I'm committed to the virtues of bravery and honesty that are required by this profession.

I take pride in what I do, but today I also take shame. I can't speak for all cops. But for me, that murder in Minnesota is the worst thing an officer can do. I can only say that I am sorry.

During the protests that followed, I've stood on that thin blue line, not out of pride but of duty, protecting the city. On that skirmish line, I've heard protestors call some of my brothers (the black officers) "Uncle Tom." And worse. Yet I know these men and women to be good people.

For the Fisher-Paulsons, it is even more complex. Even in San Francisco, there aren't a lot of families in which the son is Black and the father is a white cop.

It's tricky. Even though I'm in my own queer minority, I can never be sure that I'm not looking at an issue through the lens of white privilege.

I don't know how Zane feels. One of the boys at Thurgood Marshall called him an Oreo, and he told me it hurt deeply. And I've seen how the police in other jurisdictions have treated him. But even as a father, I cannot know the pain that he goes through.

I got a letter from a reader last week who suggested that I not mention the "Outer, Outer, Outer, Outer Excelsior" in every column. *De gustibus non disputandum est.* For us, it's the shining neighborhood on the hill. It's not perfect. It's our little corner and this is where it starts: with one family made out of mismatched parts, and each of us fails in one way or another, but we always come back together.

We are a deputy and a dancer, two teenagers and three dogs. We can't solve this complex issue. But we won't ignore it.

Here's what we try to do:

1. Think about diversity. How many of our friends are Black? LGBTQ? LatinX? What does a gathering in the Bedlam Blue Bungalow look like? Is there a Star of David on the Christmas tree?

2. Show up. Sean Dorsey once asked me, "Did you ever notice that we're all in favor of Trans rights but none of the cisgenders show up at the marches?" When Brian was the only white parent at the Black Student Union meeting, he felt awkward but he felt he had to be there.

3. Celebrate. I feel like an imposter at our Kwanzaa and Zane reminds me that he is not wearing a rainbow t-shirt at Pride this year but we all try. We have agreed that we are all Irish on Saint Patrick's Day.

4. Listen. When Aidan tells me that he is scared that he is half black and half white and not sure where he fits in, I don't try to answer the question. I just let him know I care.

5. Speak. Speak up.

6. Be nice.

I'm gonna end this with Zane's wisdom, more than a decade ago. We had gone to visit Hap, my father, in Florida. He asked us to go to his church. Hap, Hap's gay son, Hap's gay son's husband, Hap's Black grandchild, Hap's mixed-race grandchild all knelt down in his regular pew, right hand (St. Joseph's) side, back about twelve rows. Took me a minute to notice that the people to the right of us had moved away. Then the people in back. In front. To the left. In about five minutes we had three rows to ourselves. Brian scowled, and Zane asked what was going on.

"I don't know," I whispered. "Feels like some people aren't comfortable with people who are different."

"Different?" he asked.

"Yes," I still whispered. "Like Daddy being gay. Like our skin colors being different."

He grabbed my hand, and announced to the congregation, "No. Not different. Our family, we are the same. We are one."

Hap never went to that church again.

This much I know for sure: Zane's life matters.

Credo Quia Absurdum

MURPHYS, CALIFORNIA in Calaveras County has a population of 2,213 humans and 1 celebrated frog. In 1848, two brothers, John and Daniel Murphy founded Murphy's New Digging, a gold mining town, but they made more money selling goods to other miners than they ever did mining themselves. Turns out they needed that cash. The town burnt down three times (in 1859, 1874 and 1893), but survived. Nowadays it bills itself as "the Queen of the Sierra," making it the perfect vacation spot for the Fisher-Paulsons.

You can walk through the town in about ten minutes, that is if you don't stop anywhere to sample a flight of wine. Once you get to the end of the main street, you find Murphy's Old Timer Museum. On the western wall of the building there is the Wall of Comparative Ovations.

This is the kind of stuff Crazy Mike loves. It's a bunch of pictures and plaques maintained by the ancient and honorable order of E. Clampus Vitus, Grub Gulch chapter. Turns out that the clampers had their own pennant, a hoop skirt with the words, "This is the flag we fight under." Their meetings were conducted in the Hall of Comparative Ovations, mostly the backrooms of saloons that had not yet been burned down and were held "at any time before or after a full moon." Led by the First Noble Grand Humbug, the motto of this chapter is: *Credo Quia Absurdum*: Because it's absurd, I believe.

Other history in this area: it was around here that Samuel Clemens also failed as a miner and took a job as a journalist. His first big break was a short story, "The Celebrated Jumping Frog of

Calaveras County," under the pen name Mark Twain.

Into this idyllic setting came the Sasbs and the Fisher-Paulsons. The Sasbs consist of: our friend Stephanie (Sasb herself), her husband Mordecai, and her relatively neurotypical children, Elijah and Dempsey. The Fisher-Paulsons of course are: Papa, Zane, Aidan and me. Stephanie had rented a house on top of a hill, with a view as far as Yosemite. We actually have no idea what Yosemite looks like, but we reasoned that the half-domed mountain in the background must be a national park.

We did, by the way, meet one frog in the woods, although he did not demonstrate any celebrated jumping skills.

Sasb and Brian had no more ambition than to let the kids swim in the pool, while they assembled jigsaw puzzles and sampled the local viticulture. For this reason, my husband Brian is better at vacations than I am. Brian immediately takes time off as time off: once unpacked, he does not vacuum. He does not do laundry. He does not count calories. He does not get in his 10,000 steps.

Me, I still puttered. I organized the spice rack in the kitchen we rented. I still helicopter parented: *Aidan, have you finished your summer reading book? How much bug spray did you put on?* No wonder Aidan gravitated to Stephanie as she taught him how to grill hot dogs and listen for coyotes under the waxing moon.

Been happening a bit lately. The Terry Asten Bennett taught Zane how to broil hamburgers. Ms. I volunteered to teach Zane how to drive. I'm grateful for the strong women in my sons' lives, but there's a part of me that feels inadequate. At what age were they supposed to learn how to dust? How to start a barbecue? How to write thank you cards?

While these women teach my boys, they also teach me a few lessons, like how to go on vacation. Sometimes you must go away from the Outer, Outer, Outer, Outer Excelsior in order to walk away from the daily routine. Stephanie taught me that when we're on vacation, it's okay for Aidan to play on the iPad all day and eat ice cream at three in the morning.

Me, I still had to work at relaxing. So, on the second night, I cooked chili. Aidan watched as Brian and I sautéed the peppers, onions and garlic, simmered the pork, boiled the beans, crushed the tomatoes, stirred with the cinnamon stick. He watched as we made a separate vegan batch for Mordecai.

It takes two villages to raise my sons. In their teen years, they don't want to learn anything from me. It's not my job to teach Zane or Aidan how to grill a frankfurter or how to operate a stick shift. My only duty is to teach them kindness.

Quia beningus est bonum: Because it is kind it is good.

Virtual Realities

VIRTUAL REALITY costs real money.

We have two sons, Zane and Aidan. More than a year ago at a St. Patrick's party, Leah Garchik announced that whenever Adair Lara mentioned her progeny in the column, that progeny got five bucks.

My husband Brian does not demand cash when I mention him. Zane, who is sixteen going on seventeen, doesn't read my column and doesn't care.

But my younger son has the soul of an actuary. He doesn't read the column either, but scans and yells, "Ka-Ching!" every time he gets mentioned.

If Zane gets five dollars, Zane spends five dollars. My younger son however has a bank account and has not spent a single dime of it since he was first mentioned.

Which brings me back to the virtual business. When Zane graduated from eighth grade, we bought him a telephone.

We got him a basic "flip" phone for calling and nothing else. No text. No web surfing. Loving a challenge, Zane hacked into the electronics, and the next month, I opened the envelope from American Telephone and Telegraph to find a $1300 bill. More than a thousand dollars' worth of data. I think I'd have been better about the whole thing if it was something he could touch: baseball cards or sneakers or booze. But no, this was something intangible. It didn't really exist.

We disconnected his line. As I made out the check to American Telephone and Telegraph, I wondered two things:

1. Had Zane learned a lesson from this? *and*
2. Why does AT&T keep "telegraph" in their name? Do they even send telegrams anymore?

In 1825, a painter working in Washington DC on a portrait of the Marquis de Lafayette got a message that his wife was ill. He rushed home to New Haven, Connecticut to find that not only was his wife ill, but she was also dead. And buried.

He determined to find a faster way of sending communications. His name was Samuel Morse, and by May 1844, he had sent the first telegram.

Telegrams were priced by the word, so just like we now have LOL and TTYL, in those days they developed their own shorthand. The story goes that when Oscar Wilde, living in Paris, cabled his publisher in London to find out how his book was doing, he wrote, "?"

The answer was "!"

I always wanted a telegram. It seemed the kind of thing that important people got.

Turns out that American Telephone and Telegraph Company stopped sending telegrams in 1991, so why haven't they changed their name to "AT&..."?

Western Union stopped sending telegrams in 2006. There are still a few companies, like International Telegram, that will transmit them for you, but really, it's like sending a carrier pigeon or a smoke signal.

Three years have passed since the data incident. After the Zoom meeting that replaced his graduation ceremony, Papa (Brian) and I took our younger son Aidan down to get his first telephone and, what the heck, we broke down and got one for Zane as well.

Zane may or may not have learned his lesson. Fascinated by the device, he never really developed a knack for talking. He knows every text acronym and emoji, but he became enamored of punching ten numbers into a device and being able to speak live to the Terry Asten Bennett.

But Brian and I had not learned our lesson. We neglected to instill fear in our younger son. Ten days later, I got a call from my bank, fraud alert. Did I know that someone had charged $920 worth of Robux?

What are Robux? There's this free game called Roblox. People buy and sell virtual items inside this app. Only the free part runs out pretty early, and then you have to start paying for add-ons with Robux, coming straight out of Daddy's bank account.

You get it. Once again, real money to buy something that doesn't exist.

Here's the kicker: he paid me back with what I paid him for mentioning his name. Think about it: his $920 bill translated into 184 mentions of his name. And I've paid for it twice?!

My birthday is on Monday, and it too is virtual. There will be no dinner at a fancy restaurant, and I haven't bought myself a gift for the boys to give me, so I've decided that this one doesn't count. Matter of fact, long as it doesn't exist, why don't we make it my virtual 39th birthday?

And the boys can send me a telegram: "!"

Internet's End

ON THURSDAY, JULY 15, 2020, at 3:30 pm, my son Aidan announced that he had reached the end of the internet.

His journey began on March 11, 2020, when the San Francisco Archdiocese announced that Saint John's grammar school had become virtual. In those 2,547 hours, Aidan has lived, breathed and eaten Roblox, Minecraft, Words with Friends, TikTok, Uni-corny Jokes, Instagram and to quote Qoholeth, "There is nothing new under the sun." Out of all those hours surfing, he had imparted only one fact that stuck with me: some app analyzed a picture of our crippled hound Bandit and deduced that he is three-quarters Pekingese, one-quarter Japanese Chin. This explains why his bones don't fit. I'm not mentioning the name of this application because I'm not sure of its accuracy: it also calculated that I was 88% human and 11% Labrador.

Aidan's journey through the worldwide web ended with two words: "I'm bored."

He went on to complain that his summer vacation had become a stay-in-place-cation. "This pandemic isn't any fun. I would almost rather go to school."

"Life has slowed. It hasn't stopped. Let's walk," I offered.

"You and Zane are from the walking side of the family," he countered. "Me and Papa and Bandit, we like the couch." Queenie wagged her tail furiously to let us know which side she was on. Aidan pulled out one more app: turns out in the past 105 days, I've been averaging 10,986 steps a day, something along the lines of 1,153,530 steps since I first heard the term "Covid-19." And my son? An average of 1,508 steps a day, which means roughly ten trips between his bedroom ("the Brat-Cave") and the Wii in the living room. Zane may be hyphy, but Aidan is definitely loaf-y. For this reason he has a higher tolerance for boredom.

"Besides," he added, "everything is closed."

"There's a brave new world outside the quarantine of the Bedlam Blue Bungalow, if you're willing to perambulate. Even in the Outer, Outer, Outer, Outer Excelsior, there are secrets to see. Let's start small, Aidan, Cordova Market." Aidan sighed but knew that Sohel stocked Mitchell's ice cream. We put on our masks (mine was Captain America; his a wolf), put a leash on Queenie, and we strolled.

Karlotta the Fog tumbled down the San Bruno Mountain, swooping in on her boyfriend Frank the city. We shivered, turned up our sweatshirt hoods and on the first corner we saw the Roof Cow. John and Susan have let her live topside since the boys were shorter than me. The story goes that the Roof Cow is a princess-in-exile, deposed from her throne on the nearby Cow Palace in a *moo d'etat*.

Other neighborhoods have painted ladies, gold hydrants, tiled steps and windmills, but we have Bovine on a Shingle. This story is true: David Studach, one of my readers, sent a fan letter addressed: "Roof Cow, Outer, Outer, Outer, Outer Excelsior, San Francisco" and it got there.

Two blocks more, as we skirted McLaren Park we saw La Grande. Likely, you've seen it yourself, from 280. It's that eighty-foot tall aquamarine water tank, the poor man's Coit Tower. You can get there by the Philosopher's Way. I've lived here for twenty years and I still haven't found all fourteen stones in the only trail built for philosophers in the United States. Took me three tries to find the Jerry Garcia amphitheater.

We strolled by the bocce courts as the carillon of Epiphany Church rang "O Sanctissima." And I told Aidan that when we walked, we had time to wonder: like I don't know why there are totem poles in Cayuga Park. I don't know why the coyote always stops to meet me at the top of South Hill Boulevard. I don't know if Wonder Woman ever lived on Amazon Street.

By the time we walked back, the sun was setting. The foghorn moaned far away. Thanks to Karlotta, we could not see Neo-Wise Comet, the first astral body to be named after my mother: Nurse Vivian Wise. And so it remained another puzzle.

I put my arm around Aidan's shoulder, "There are some things that you are supposed to enjoy because you don't know the answer."

"Like how you're part Labrador?" he asked.

Here's the point, Aidan. You may have traveled all four corners of the internet, but you will never run out of San Francisco. It is like a treasure hunt. Get out of the house. Put on a mask. Stay six feet apart. There's a mystery around every corner.

Kitchen Magic

JULY 20TH was the anniversary of my 39th Birthday. Brother XX looked up the date on a calendar website and informed me that I was not listed and therefore not famous. Interestingly enough, it said that this was the day of birth for Gregor Mendel, Carlos Santana, Sir Edmund Hillary and Diana Rigg. As I've accomplished nothing in the fields of Genetics, Latin American jazz, mountain climbing or avenging, I expect I would need to work a little harder.

Fame is not one of my ambitions, although it does tickle Zane's fancy. Last Sunday, we returned from Cliff's Variety by way of Dolores. The car next to us honked, and I assumed that I'd committed a wrong-of-way, but the couple smiled and asked, "Is this the Kipcap? Is that Zane?" Zane loved this because not only would it get his name mentioned in the column (thus earning five bucks) but it also allowed him celebrity status.

Me, I'm famous only to my dogs Buddyboy, Bandit and Queenie, for my skill at dropping bacon on the kitchen floor when Brian's not looking.

I'm unknown except perhaps for Aunt Dee and Uncle Howard, who live in Concord. There's no blood relation. But they are famous to us, and we are infamous to them. Our connection is that Aunt Dee's sister served in the Air Force with Brian's father. In 1991, Brian and I moved to California on a dare, knowing no one who lived west of the Mississippi. But Aunt Dee invited us to Thanksgiving dinner, announced that we were family. If the Fisher-Paulsons have a matriarch, it is Aunt Dee.

Last weekend, she invited us out so the boys could swim in the pool, while we adults socially distanced a barbecue. While Brian and I sat under the plum tree, Uncle Howard taught Zane how to grill steaks and Aunt Dee served up five-layer dip and corn on the cob. After dinner, she announced, "Well, I intended on a beautiful white cake with chocolate frosting and coconut for your birthday. But after I took it out of the oven, I noticed some of the batter hadn't cooked, so I scooped that out, and tried to cover the gaps with icing, but… well… you'll see."

She retrieved it from the kitchen, and sure enough this was Betty Crocker on a bad day. She had also forgotten candles, and so there was a mozzarella stick planted in the middle. I tried to blow out the mozzarella, but really, you can't blow out the cheese, you can only cut it.

Took a picture of it (Say cheese!) and the cake turned out to be moist and kind of fun. Kitchen magic. The next day Zane and Aidan surprised me with an M&M cake. And the next day, Aunt Amanda surprised me with a gnome cake. So really, my weekend was perfect, except for the lack of candle.

There are things I cannot talk about in this column, for either legal reasons or the psychologists telling me that I had already given the boys enough to talk about in therapy.

But I can talk about candles.

It's a Catholic thing. My Jewish friends get it. My Protestant friends don't get it, and my atheist friends think I'm quaint but deluded. The pagans really get it.

There's a candle in the window of the Bedlam Blue Bungalow in the Outer, Outer, Outer, Outer Excelsior. We've kept a flame burning on the porch since July 14, 2018. There are full moons, stars and comets in the violet night over the San Bruno Mountains, but this taper lights the way home.

And even though I buy it in the Lucky Candle on Geneva and Mission, I don't think it has any powers. Not really. As Tim would say, it's kitchen magic: its only power is the intent. We strike a match. The porch glows brighter. We meditate. We think of family.

It's also a Jewish thing. Burton Kranzel followed my column for the last few years of his life and was my candle whisperer. He'd write things like, "I woke up at 2:10 am to one of those middle of the night instant awake moments, and knew I was supposed to light my lantern for the Fisher-Paulsons. I visualized them all together."

He passed away last April, so he never saw that we'd gotten back together, at least for the most part. But he believed in us, and taught us to believe in ourselves.

This year it does not matter what was blown out. It matters only what we intend.

Pure Oxygen

M Y OFFICE in the Sheriff's Department is tucked away in a corner and has no windows, but it has a skylight. I'd gotten to work early, sifted through e-mails. 6:51, I heard sirens in the background, but that's not unusual for South of Market Street. Felt a little warm.

And then I heard a yell, "We're evacuating!" Part of me thought, "Who's pulling a drill at 6:51 in the morning?" The other part snapped my gun into the holster, clicked on the radio and checked door by door that people were getting out.

We cleared the building in minutes and hit the door. Fire engulfed the six buildings around us, flames reaching three stories in the air. Black smoke billowed, and ash smudged down in flakes. The heat came in waves. We moved out ammunition, evacuated cars out of the lot, and set up incident command.

And if you think deputies are brave, more than a hundred firefighters drove their trucks up and got out their hoses. More than a hundred million gallons of water rained down that block.

Crazy Mike showed up, making sure that everyone had coffee and a bagel. This is Crazy Mike. He let it slip that he stashed "emergency cash" in his gun locker (which may or may not have been on fire) so that Mrs. Crazy Mike didn't know about it, but he's not worried because, "All the humans are safe. What's inside that building are only objects."

I tried to be Zen, but I had a lot of objects in that office, including ten uniforms, four pairs of boots, three utility belts, a laptop, Alex

Ross comic art and antique batmobiles.

There are two framed paintings in my office. My son Zane drew the first when he was in kindergarten, a portrait of me as a ninja cop, looking just a little like Edvard Munch's "Scream". The other Aidan had drawn after I visited Saint John's School for career day, me wearing the Stetson hat, with the caption, "He is responsible for 182 deputies and takes care of the deer and mountain lions." This was the one and only A that Aidan ever got in elementary school. I said to Crazy Mike, "I know that they're only objects, but right now they're the objects I miss most."

I called my husband Brian and he asked if we were all safe. I told him that I was okay. I said I was sorry about losing all those objects in the fire and he said, "Well, at least you know what next week's column will be about."

Here were the best parts of the day:

1. This was the first time that I ever got pure oxygen! Turns out that it's just like air, only cooler.

2. After the fire was mainly out, the firefighters let us into the building to grab a few essential objects. We waded through about six inches of standing water, but got out some expensive equipment. Smoke filled the hallway, but Rob, one of the firefighters followed me when I made a dash for my office. I grabbed the two paintings, and Rob said, "Well, we got to get your Captain America shield out too." And we ran into the misty air of San Francisco, and really, I was grateful just to breathe and to whatever force in the universe that had reunited me with those objects.

Long hours later, I drove home. Brian and Aidan came and hugged me. I opened the car and showed them the two drawings. Brian almost teared up, as did I, but Aidan glanced sideways in what I recognized as his guilty look.

"What?" I asked.

"Dad, you do know that Maliya drew that picture. I just wanted you to think that I had an A."

There's a lesson there somewhere: the object you save from a five-alarm fire might turn out to be some other child's A.

Raising Two Dads

WHEN MY BOOK *A Song for Lost Angels*: *How Daddy and Papa Fought to Save Their Family* got nominated for a Benjamin Franklin independent publishing award in 2015, there was a minor uptick in sales. For one week it was in the Top Ten in books about parenting on Amazon.

Parenting? I don't know what genre I expected the book to be in. Is it a Romance? Memoir? LGBTQ? Science Fiction?

Brother X was horrified. "Kevin knows as much about parenting as he does about running a three-ring circus," he joked.

He's right. But you know what? Love your clowns and the rest will follow.

In 1946 Doctor Benjamin Spock published **On Parenting** and as sufficient as that was, maybe I'll write my own, but not so much on how to *father* as how to *family*. As much as we raise our boys, they too are raising their dads.

The boys have started checking up on me: They say "Put on your seatbelt. Stay in the crosswalk." Zane's taller than me by almost a head, so when he volunteers to carry the groceries, I let him.

This past summer when neither son had to be anywhere at any given time, I still needed to go to bed by 9:30 p.m. to be in time for morning muster.

It started as a joke: the boys took turns telling me a bedtime story about a misfit family, whose names were Enaz, Nadia, Yddad and Apap, and how along with their magical flying rescue dogs,

Tidnab, Yddubyob, and Eineeuq. they found their way to a bungalow in the fictional Inner, Inner, Inner, Inner Roislecxe. When they ran out of stories, it became riddles and/or just questions. As I drifted into sleep, Aidan asked me, "Daddy, when you wake up, does the dream go on without you?" I still don't know the answer.

Which brings me to CHAPTER ONE of the book I would write: You don't win with authority. Authority lasts only until your back is turned. You better have influence.

Nurse Vivian got away with a fair amount of, "Because I said so." That doesn't work with my boys. Each came with special conditions, and Zane's was an inability to say yes. Aidan simply must know how things work. I cannot tell him to separate the lights from the darks in the laundry, "because I said so." Instead he demands the history of bleach, and debates why we needed to launder when Aidan likes his clothes a little dirty.

CHAPTER TWO: Be present.

CHAPTER THREE: Influence doesn't always work. My husband Brian insists that my charm does not work on teenagers, it only embarrasses them. So, if you don't have influence, use trickery. Here's how I toilet-trained Zane: I threw Cheerios in the bowl and challenged him that I had better aim.

CHAPTER FOUR: Children are not problems. They are challenges. We do our best to avoid schools where they claim that one of our sons is difficult. We prefer the term "spirited." I don't know what the bungalow would be like if there were normal people in it. I do know all four of us have challenges, and the way we overcome them makes us better.

For example, Aidan has an eating "challenge." So, to get food into him, some nights we have snacky dinners and some nights we have Sundae Mondays, which means eat whatever you want as long as you put hot fudge on top.

CHAPTER FIVE: You can either choose to be right or choose to be happy. My husband's better at this than me, and here's his advice: You can either beat your son at "Words with Friends," or you can teach him to enjoy the game.

LAST CHAPTER (for now): There's only one lesson you must teach your child: be kind.

Waking Up Early

ALL AT ONCE it is September.

Fogust is one of my favorite months. Let the Yankees have the dog days. In fact, let them have the cat nights. We have the fog days of summer. Felt a little betrayed by this summer: months of sheltering in place; social unrest; lightning strikes that ignited more than three hundred fires that burnt people's lives down, and leaving us all breathing ash; the season of virtual Giants and zoom not-quite-happy hours.

Friday night was hot, that sticky kind, and the fan in our window only stirred the sooty haze.

Some mornings I'm not enthusiastic about leaving the bed and Saturday morning is my time to sleep in. But at 6:22 am, our oldest dog, Buddyboy put his paw on my bladder, which meant we both had to get up and find relief in the bathroom. Barefoot, I carried him out to the yard only to find that the lawn was damp. It was no longer hot. It no longer smelled of smoke. There were no stars, only silver mist, swirling around the "ticky tacky little boxes on the hillside." I would've kissed the fog if she would let me.

I went back and picked up Bandit, who joined Buddyboy on the lawn with less enthusiasm. Then I got Queenie, and there is no creature more enthusiastic about peeing on wet grass than a 9-month-old-mostly-Pekingese puppy.

The point is I chose not to be miserable about waking up before the sun rose. I chose to enjoy the dawn.

What's the secret? Getting up on the right side of the bed. Know where the expression "getting up on the wrong side of the bed" came from? The Romans. They did not much like the port side. In fact, the Latin term for left-handed was sinister. And so, getting up on the left side of the bed meant that you invited bad luck into your day.

For thirty-four years, I have slept on the right side of the bed, but I realize to my husband Brian, that would mean stage left.

He, by the way, slept through all this bliss, as did my son Aidan. But not Zane. Waking up early meant just the two of us on the drive to the psychic Starbucks on Portola.

We came back the long way, along Glen Canyon. "What did you dream about last night?" Zane asked as he took a sip of his hot chocolate, with extra whipped cream.

I tipped my seven-pump chai tea latte towards him: "I dreamt I was on this little strip of land, a hillside between two streets, like Baltimore Street, and in the grass lived these little people, pixies or leprechauns, I wasn't sure. Anyway, I realized that I had to feed and clothe them, and I couldn't figure out where to buy clothes for an elf. American Doll? House of Barbie?"

"Dad, you do realize that you don't get any rest when you sleep? That you're always figuring out a problem? Waking up must be a relief."

He's correct. When the dream ends, the dream begins. It brings a Bedlam Blue Bungalow in the Outer, Outer, Outer, Outer Excelsior, a land of Monkey Puzzle trees and Coyote Mint bushes blooming pointed pink flowers.

We drove past the bovine on the roof. Her name is Ruth Cow, and according to Susan Reichardt, she's a Holstein. According to the nearby Cow Palace, she's in exile. We drove past the stuffed armadillo in a box on the last Saturday before Back-to-Virtual-School.

As we got out of the car, me carrying Papa's skinny cinnamon dolce and Zane carrying Aidan's hot chocolate, he said, "By the way, that session I attended this summer? Turns out I'm graduating from high school on time."

Miracles happen. In the meantime, wake up with the right attitude (even if you are sleeping stage left). It's not a matter of wellness. It's a matter of swellness.

Ode to Our Socks

O N A SATURDAY MORNING, my mother, Nurse Vivian, sat on our couch upholstered in a black nylon found only in the 1960s. She labored over a wool sock on the darning egg, five other socks in the on-deck position.

She herself wore hosiery, mostly white to go with her uniform, but with three rowdy sons and an equally careless husband, holes in the toes were a regular thing. The aluminum door swung open. Brother X, Brother XX and I burst in: "Look! See what Hap (our father) bought!"

Nurse Vivian put down her sewing needle, walked down the stoop and looked at our red Chevrolet station wagon. Tied to the top was an aluminum rowboat.

There wasn't a lot of boating in South Ozone Park, Queens. Coney Island was at the other end of the F Train, and no one rowed there.

Nurse Vivian walked back inside, came back out, handed Hap the six torn garments, and said, "Now that we've got our own yacht, we don't need to darn socks. Ever. Again."

Socks are not a recent invention. Archaeologists found a red pair near the Nile River dating back to somewhere around 250 to 420 B.C.E. The Greeks loved them. In fact, the word "sock" comes from the Greek word *sykchos*, or slipper.

Theirs were made from matted animal furs. I've tried unsuccessfully to duplicate this process with Queenie, Buddyboy and

Bandit, but those of you who've tried to shave a Pekingese know how poorly that turns out for both shaver and shavee.

Without socks we'd have nothing to hang on the chimney with care. It's the only garment to have two national sports teams too. They don't have the Boston Red Jodhpurs or the Chicago White Jocks.

Counterintuitive, but my husband, Brian, is the one who wears the superhero socks, nylon and in bright colors. My son Zane wears whatever he can steal from Brian, grabbing any two, mismatched, and they become fashion: "Black Panther"-themed on the left, argyle on the right.

My son Aidan has stopped wearing socks altogether, but I've warned him that Riordan High School is not a commando environment. Then again, Albert Einstein refused to wear socks, even when he was awarded the Nobel Prize. I can't wait to see what Aidan will do with relativity.

Me, I'm the Pablo Neruda of the family. As he wrote in the famous *Ode to My Socks*, "What is good is doubly good when it is a matter of two socks made of wool in winter."

Few things make me happier than taking off my work boots and changing into a pair of warm, thick socks. My favorite pair was a blue hiker's merino that I bought in a sockporium that no longer exists in the Stonestown Galleria. I named the left one Bert, the right one Ernie.

I wore Bert and Ernie every Saturday for five years. Every soccer game that Zane or Aidan ever played was witnessed by these socks.

And then one laundry day, Bert was gone.

According to a 2016 report by Samsung, the average person loses 15 socks per year, or 1,264 socks over a lifetime. I've never understood the term "a pair of underwear" but I accept that socks are pairs, like swans. They mate for life, and if one goes early, the other is lost.

Ernie took it hard. To this day he sits in the bottom drawer, between the sachet and Tommy Johns, hoping that when that dryer burns out, Bert will be found in a vent or lint trap.

Before Crazy Mike asks, "What's the moral?" let me state: The Fisher-Paulsons in the Outer, Outer, Outer, Outer Excelsior are a family of mismatched socks: crews, no-shows, bobby sox and leg warmers. One's a little frayed in the gusset. One has lost its elastic. One has an anxiety disorder.

One got lost in the wash, but we never gave up on it. One late December it reappeared. Faith starts out in your feet.

Lack of Pride

LET ME WARN YOU: this is a soapbox column.

On September 2, 2019, the San Francisco Pride Board announced that "We cannot welcome the participation of the San Francisco Police Department's Pride Alliance — which is to say, uniformed SFPD officers, marching as a pride contingent." The statement was signed "Queer Solidarity forever." But is banishment really solidarity?

The minute you start kicking people out of the revolution, you've lost the revolution.

I reached out to President of the Board Carolyn Wysinger for clarification, and she referred me to Peter Kane, the Communications Director. He let me know that the ban occurred "because of a widespread community outcry over the inadequate response from SFPD and the city's Department of Police Accountability over an episode of police violence at Pride 2019."

And I get their disagreement with the DPA, but is taking it out against the LGBTQ2 officers the solution? Excluding the cops on our side?

And whereas the SFPD are not allowed to march, they *will* be protecting the public safety at the event.

I've been marching for 38 years, back when it was a dangerous thing to do, getting tomatoes and bottles thrown at us. And the cops didn't always protect us.

In fact, Pride was born out of an opposition to prejudiced police officers both at Stonewall in New York, and Compton's Cafeteria in San Francisco. And years later, in 1990, a few of the bravest women I knew convinced me to join with them in the Pink Panther Patrol, a neighborhood watch group who defended the LGBTQ2 community in Greenwich Village against bashing.

Here's the story of why I earned a badge: that same year, I was living in Jersey City with Brian, long before we had the right to be married. Late one night, I walked to the mailbox wearing a "Read My Lips" t-shirt, adorned with a picture of two sailors kissing in the middle of Kennedy Boulevard. A teenager whispered "F—t" and a dozen of his friends kicked and punched me. I still have a scar on my forehead.

The cops didn't come that night. Brian came to the rescue, wearing a silk caftan shirt and carrying a baseball bat.

The next day I went to the precinct, still wearing the t-shirt. A desk cop looked up from his typewriter, "Don't you think maybe you were asking for it, wearing that?"

"You can't say that," I said.

"Buddy, if I had a nickel for every f—t that got socked in this neighborhood, I'd be retired," he said. "You think my job is easy, you try doing it."

So, I did. Santa Rosa Police Academy tried everything to make me quit: accidental baton strikes to my forehead, putting nails in my tires and the gun range instructors letting me know that "accidents happen on the range..."

And a straight sheriff named Mike Hennessy backed me all the way.

Twenty-seven years later, I'm a chief deputy, one of a few LGBTQ2 officers in the country to reach that rank. And I made it not by being gay but by being good.

Because I have a seat at the table, I'm part of the change. The San Francisco Sheriff's Office, for example, was an early leader in AIDS education. The Office developed the first Transgender Awareness class for the Peace Officer Standards of Training.

When we LGBTQ2 became peace officers, we began to change them. Yes, there's even farther to go. Yes, I know some knuckleheads, but I know ten times as many decent women and men who take that oath seriously: that their "fundamental duty is to protect the innocent against oppression."

Over the years, straight deputies joined us in the Pride March because it was the right thing to do.

Paradoxically, the San Francisco Pride Committee discriminates against LGBTQ2 officers today. It's like taking the list away from Schindler because he was raised Catholic.

When my black son walks hand-in-hand with me in my uniform along Market Street, it means we have found common ground. I've seen people weep. THIS is how we win the revolution, proving that we all can be a part of making change happen, proving that it's all colors in the rainbow flag.

We won't get to walk down Market Street this year. Leave that to the corporations and the straight politicians hustling for votes.

But Brian, Zane, Aidan, Buddyboy, Bandit and Queenie, we'll march the Outer, Outer, Outer, Outer Excelsior. And in that we'll take our own pride.

In human solidarity forever.

The Coral Anniversary

O N MY SIDE of the family, a long-lasting marriage is genetic. Nurse Vivian and Hap were married 54½ years. On Brian's side, however, marriage was more of a blood sport. They didn't have in-laws. They had "out-laws".

His Aunt Jeannie is one example. Monmouth, Maine, is not a big town, population of 4,129, according to 2018 data from the United States Census Bureau. Around the time she got her sixth divorce, Aunt Jeannie calculated she had an ex-family member in one out of three households. She ran out of clergymen willing to officiate.

After Brian's mother divorced his father, Jerry, he went on to wed seven more times. His penultimate wife, Aloise, introduced him to his last, Edna, saying, "One more and we got a baseball team."

It was, therefore, highly unlikely that Brian would stay with me as long as he has. When we first met, he was a Broadway dancer, whereas I sold dinnerware in downtown Newark.

My cousin Rita introduced us over lasagna at her apartment in Jersey City in 1985. Even she said, "It's like Fred Astaire and Archie Bunker." But against all odds it worked.

This year marked the coral anniversary of when we first met. Nothing says "I love you" quite like marine invertebrates. It was once thought that red coral protects against pestilence, so considering the plague we've had lately, maybe the timing is right.

What's our secret to happiness for all these years?

1. We're the classic western romance. Brian's the dance hall girl. I'm the deputy. He doesn't make me tango, and I don't make him arrest criminals.

2. We didn't rush into marriage. The fact that it was illegal at the time may have contributed, but on September 19, 1987, in a little bar in Chelsea, Brian and I exchanged rings in front of a priest. His job with the Catholic Church didn't last much longer, but Brian and I lasted the next 33 years and counting. In Germany that's the tin anniversary, but in France it's the porphyry anniversary (*myweddinganniversary.com*). Had to look that one up. Porphyry is a crystal rock made of feldspar. After a third of a century, nothing says "I love you" quite like cooled magma.

3. We don't switch anniversary dates. We became domestic partners on September 19, 1991. We got legally married on September 19, 2008. That would officially make this our twelfth anniversary, traditionally pearl, but Brian never cast pearls before wine. I wrote to Hallmark to ask for the *gay* anniversary list: Which year is gym memberships, and which Beyonce tickets?

4. We don't stay together for the children. But I do think that Zane and Aidan stay together for the sake of their parents. If brothers could divorce, Aidan would file for palimony.

5. We might be staying together for the sake of the dogs, who are much more loyal than our children. Queenie never complains about homework. Bandit never skips class, unlike Aidan who managed to be the first student at Riordan to earn virtual detention.

6. We still make each other laugh. It's not a Dad joke. It's a Husband joke, which means that it's even lamer.

Whenever anyone asks me how long Brian and I have been together, I say, "35 years. And it feels like 35 minutes…" I clasp Brian's hand. He smiles and adds, "Under. Water."

We still argue over who drives worse (he does). We still live in the Bedlam Blue Bungalow in the Outer, Outer, Outer, Outer Excelsior because that's our home. He still slouches in all of our pictures together so that people will think I'm the tall one.

We've made up our own family: sons and puppies, aunts and uncles, in-laws and "out-laws."

Oh, yeah. And love. That's the real secret.

Vote, Seriously

I'M ASKING YOU TO VOTE.

My husband and I do it at Guadalupe Elementary School. We bring the boys. We celebrate the republic.

If you follow this column, you know how I'm going to vote in November. But that's not today's issue. This column doesn't appear in the editorial section for a reason. We're about family, not politics. But this week's column isn't about my ballot; it's about yours.

Zane's school got evacuated in the Glass Fire. The good part of this year's fifth crisis is that he's home again, learning to cook. He can flip a burger and fry a chicken.

We get to sit at the dining room table, say grace and toast "the best boys in the world." Lately, we've clinked glasses with Martinelli's sparkling cider instead of milk. We had six bottles that we had been saving for a special occasion only to realize that the four of us being together in the Bedlam Blue Bungalow in the Outer, Outer, Outer, Outer Excelsior was all the occasion we needed.

Aidan still takes about an hour to eat one hot dog and that gives us time to talk. We used to argue over who would win in a fight between Superman and Ben 10. But lately he's been bringing up things he saw on the internet. Did I know that Tarzan was Elsa's (*Frozen*) younger brother? Did I know that you can see a dead munchkin in *The Wizard of Oz*?

Another case of "fake news" online. This was how we got to politics. Zane turned 17 in August, meaning that this is the last election in which he won't be eligible to vote.

One of his online classes is Civics, so we know that in the fifth century B.C.E., the Greeks took democracy seriously. In fact, if an adult citizen didn't participate, they'd drag a rope dipped in red paint around them, marking them for their absence. This may be what we mean by getting roped in.

The Athenians voted by putting a pebble into one of two jars. The word ballot comes from the French *ballote,* or small ball.

"Why do you take voting so seriously?" Zane asked us.

We vote for a lot of reasons, partly because not voting leads to heartbreak and partly because I don't drink bourbon.

During the 1980 election, I attended the University of Michigan and lived in a cooperative with a young Republican. We had argued right up until the results started coming in.

He said, "I tell you what. I'll take a shot of Wild Turkey for every state that (Jimmy) Carter wins. You take a shot for every (Ronald) Reagan state." I never made it past Kansas.

We vote because even when we don't respect the winner, we respect the process.

We vote because voting means sitting down for Lo Mein and Pork Buns, arguing about every measure on the ballot. In San Francisco, which I sometimes refer to as the city of silly propositions, citizens voted in 1993 on the question: "Should a police officer get to walk his beat with a ventriloquist's dummy?"

We vote because I'm in charge of the deputies who pick up the ballots. Don't let anyone tell you that the vote's not safe. In San Francisco, we treat that duty as sacred.

Zane, I'm not going to say I don't care about how you'll vote, because I do. Just don't get your "fake news" on the internet like Aidan.

But I care more that you do indeed vote. We vote because in

the last presidential election 138 million people voted, only 58.1% of those who were eligible. That means almost a hundred million non-voters left money on the table. As my mother, Nurse Vivian, said, "If you don't vote, you can't bitch."

October 19 is the deadline to register to vote in California.

Vote, because the truth has its own engine.

Seriously, just vote.

Queenie Speaks

THE MIST still swirled at two in the afternoon on Thursday, a cool breeze swirling down Canyon Drive. Broom trees bloomed in bright fuchsia, the perfect weather for a walk. But Queenie, our youngest dog, was not content.

It was just Buddyboy, Queenie and me who ventured outside that day. Bandit's legs don't work so well, so he skips the longer promenades.

Queenie has milk-white fur, with patches of black and chestnut, including a circle around her left eye that makes her look like the Tareyton cigarette smoker who'd rather fight than switch brands. She was born on December 9, 2019, which makes her a Sagittarius. My husband Brian calls her the most spoiled Pekingese this side of the Boxer Rebellion.

There's a legend that the Pekingese was born when Buddha shrunk a lion to the size of a dog. Two thousand years in lineage later, they're one of the oldest breeds known to humankind.

"Still," Queenie insisted, "We may have been domesticated but we have never been tamed."

"Why can't I write my own column?" Queenie complained to Buddyboy. "You wrote one in April 2018. Bandit wrote one July 2018! Zane and Aidan get $5 every time their name is mentioned. What do we get? Kibble!"

Buddyboy, her biscuit-colored adoptive uncle, looked up from checking his pee-mail, "Well first of all, you need to know how to write." He wagged his tail, checked another California lilac, "And second of all, you need to know how to speak human."

"Human?" Queenie responded.

"Yes, you know the gibberish that Daddy, the guy on the other end of the leash, speaks. But trust me, you're not getting into the San Francisco Chronicle, the Voice of the West, without speaking a little human. Maybe you could learn on Barkolingo." Buddyboy paused, scratched his chin with his good back leg and asked, "Besides, what would you write about?"

"Well, the vice-presidential debate last night for one. I mean, why make a fuss about the running mates, when really, it's the walking mates that matter?" Queenie professed. "Humans are pretty silly if you ask me. In the debates, they argue but never get anywhere."

"Not like us dogs," she added earnestly. "We bark, we growl, and then we sniff each other's butts. It's much more civilized."

"But who would Major debate?" Buddyboy countered. Major is the German Shepherd who chose the Bidens in 2018 (not the first hound to choose the vice president).

On the Republican side, Donald Trump was the first president in a century not to have a pet, which may be the problem.

Fala (Franklin D. Roosevelt), Checkers (Richard Nixon) and Bo (Barack Obama) were the most famous canines to live in the White House. But John Quincy Adams kept a pet alligator, a gift of the Marquis de Lafayette. James Buchanan kept an elephant. Teddy Roosevelt, who famously had a Teddy bear, also had a zebra.

We had reached the downhill part of the walk with a view of the LaGrande Water Tank and, even farther along, the S.F. Tower almost obscured in the midday fog. Buddyboy shrugged, "The way I see it, there are only three presidents who have ever gotten impeached; two of them had no pets and the third had a … cat."

According to the National Pet Owners Survey, 63.4 million dogs haven chosen to live with American families, or about 62 percent of all households.

"But whatever you do," Buddyboy said while sniffing at a butterfly, "never discuss politics with Cheddar (the cat who lives next door). I am, after all, a yellow dog democrat, and Jon Carroll is right: all cats vote Republican."

When we arrived back home, a Bedlam Blue Bungalow in the Outer, Outer, Outer, Outer Excelsior, Buddyboy jumped through the dog door with plans for the rest of the day: "Let's go inside, Queenie. I'll teach you how to type."

Our Therapy Graduation

THE FISHER-PAULSONS graduated therapy on Wednesday, October 14th: three years to finish a year-long course.

This was not our first trip to therapy world. Back in the 70s, Nurse Vivian took me to my first analyst. I'm not sure if she was trying to "cure" me, but the therapist didn't blink. He talked to me for fifteen minutes before he said, "Mrs. Paulson, this isn't the right time for therapy for Kevin. If you, however, have a few minutes to talk, I think Kevin would show significant progress."

I went back for both of my midlife crises, and then came the boys. Since Zane was about two years old, we've seen seven psychiatrists and twenty-two therapists — and only three of them left the field after working with us.

One appointment lasted forty-nine minutes, leading my husband Brian to comment, "Your blind dates lasted longer."

In our first family therapy, the leader made us draw pictures of the family as animals. Whereas my husband Brian got drawn as an owl, a panther, a unicorn and dragon, respectively, all four of us depicted me as a dog.

Then we did superheroes. Turns out Brian's the masked marvel. I'm the sidekick.

So, this is not our first psychoanalysis — and it won't be our last. It's more like graduation from middle school therapy.

Aidan was the valedictorian, Zane the salutatorian. Brian earned a diploma with a major in patience. Buddyboy, Bandit and Queenie have support dog status. Me I graduated *sine laude,* no honor whatsoever. Instead of degrees we got diagnoses.

After the appointment, we stuffed our faces with Mitchell's Ice Cream to celebrate, a smorgasbord that started with Grasshopper Pie and ended with Dulce de Leche. Oreos in mint ice cream for dinner might not seem normal, but that's not what we were shooting for. We were celebrating that we were brave enough to ask for help and brave enough to see it through.

We celebrated the wins, the lessons learned:

1. Know when you're in over your head. At some point we all lose it. For me, it was probably the afternoon that Aidan got his head stuck in a staircase, but each of us gets to give up at some point.
2. It's okay to phone a friend. The friend will remind you how much you love your children. But know this: Your friends will have sympathy, but not answers.
3. This isn't the measles. You don't have it one week and then never again.
4. But remember that, like the measles, none of you chose to have this issue.
5. Don't judge. This rule applies to you readers.

Twenty years ago, I was one of those "Why-can't-that-mother-keep-her-child-quiet-on-the-airplane" people. Time has humbled me.

I've been the parent standing in the middle of the street with a son lying down in a San Francisco intersection, and I know all the reasons we were there were invisible. The Chief of Police herself tried to get him out, but he wouldn't budge.

Next time you see a child screaming while throwing a bowl of spaghetti at Olive Garden, do not assume that the father/mother is a failure. Assume that she/he is doing their best. And when you yourself are the parent sitting on the curb watching your son and the Chief of Police argue, remember the words of Oscar Wilde, "We are all of us in the gutter, but some of us are looking at the stars."

6. The first six rounds of therapy don't count.

7. A teenager's resentment has a very short shelf life.

8. Lower your expectations. Don't focus on wanting your child to go to Notre Dame, become a doctor or reinvent the laws of physics. Instead, strive for your child to be happy.

Last lesson, for now: Children don't remember lessons, but they will remember love.

Breakfast in America

M Y HUSBAND BRIAN sleeps in late, as does Zane. Aidan naps
lightly until he can sneak his iPad into his bedroom around 4
am. So at 6:22 am, when Bandit's legs don't work very well, I carry
him out to our teeny yard. Buddyboy runs out to mark whatever bush
Bandit has just marked, giving me time to grab Queenie off the bed.
She swoons in my arms, and the four of us stand in the mist, listening
to the rustle of the golden amber leaves. A dove coos in the California
lilac. We walk back in, I change the dogs' water, and brew myself
tea. These five minutes of quiet are the best part of the day. Don't tell
my husband, but some days when we break the fast, we break our
diet: donuts.

This column gets turned in long before Tuesday night, so I'm
writing to you from the far side of the election. From where I type I
cannot tell if it's a landslide or a nail biter; whether the house is red
or blue; who may have declared victory. I can tell you only this: it's
morning in America.

And whether it's morning in America or we are mourning in
America, dawn comes a lot earlier this week, thanks to the wisdom of
Benjamin Franklin. At some point, people voted on daylight savings.
Somebody lost that vote. Somebody won. Okay, the omnisicient
copy editors will remind me so I might as well tell you that the first
vote took place in 1918, when it was passed because farm products
are better when gathered with dew on.

Elections have consequences. Except when they don't. Two

years ago, 60% of Californians voted to have daylight savings time year round, but it never happened because the federal government declined to give us permission to make a time change.

This presidential campaign, however, has gone on for four years, and the next campaign begins at noon.

During the last week, my husband and I scrutinized the mailers that urged us to vote one way or another on propositions. When Supervisor Asha Safai dropped by the Bedlam Blue Bungalow and asked for my vote, I felt pretty good about democracy until an ad popped up in my Facebook feed that read, "Make them pay." This made me sad because it was for a cause that I usually supported. I miss the days when politicians shook hands and kissed babies.

Maybe it's the pandemic. Maybe it's Russian interference, but this year it feels like politics have been set on screech. Everyone's shrieking that the sky is falling and it's the other party's fault.

Now I'm not perfect either. I've been caught yelling French curse words at the television, but I have Zane to save my soul. "Dad, you know this guy has a son? You know his wife loves him? You do know he doesn't speak French?"

Whether elephant or donkey, you have lost the election if you have lost your compassion. You may care deeply about who occupies the White House, but care just as much about who sleeps in a tent on Duboce.

Care that black lives matter. Care that no human is illegal. Care that love is love.

Elections have consequences, but issues are not people.

Those of you who read this column know that the Outer, Outer, Outer, Outer Excelsior is the shining city on the hill. When the sun sneaks over the San Bruno mountains this morning, let it shine on an America that is merciful. When we wake up, forgive the crazy uncle who canceled out your vote. In fact, ask him over for a cup of coffee. Make bacon and eggs. Or better yet donuts. This is the way we can make America great again. With kindness.

It's not just morning again in America. It's breakfast in America.

Dad-D

AT SOME POINT, the D falls off the Dad.
My son Aidan had a speech deficit, but the only way anyone would notice it these days is in his pronunciation of double
consonants. He breaks them in two, thus rendering kitten into "kitten" and bunny into "bun-knee." And so, for fifteen years he has called
me Dad-D.

But something shifted in the past few months and he now calls
me Dad. In fact, Brian and I are no longer Dad-D and Pop-Pa. We are
the Dads.

A lot gets thrown out with that D. It feels like a step down. When
my sons called me Daddy, I could boogie the Snacky Dinner dance at
Safeway, and both Zane and Aidan joined in. Now they pretend they
don't know me.

There was a time when Aidan was proud to be my electronics
whisperer. When I'd be writing this column and the iMac crashed,
he would be the one to find the column in the ether. But now, he just
rolls his eyes and says, "You were probably just going to tell the head
stuck in the staircase story again."

When I laugh or sneeze too loudly, I get "the look." Without a
word, I can feel it say: "Really? You don't have a volume control on
your nose, Dad?"

Zane also grew into an eye-rolling champion and doesn't hesitate
to point out when I've told the same "Dad joke" more than once.
When I say "drat" Aidan asks, "Can't you just say 'Damn' like other

fathers?" And hugging in front of teenage peers? Impossible.

I adjust. I text from the kitchen that dinner is ready. I no longer expect them in the living room to watch *Avatar*. I don't have to like it, but I still have to love them.

My own father must have gone through this during my teen brat years. At some point, right around the time that we disagreed about "*Star Wars*" and "Disco Inferno," I dropped Dad-D entirely and started calling him Hap.

It was his nickname when he was a lieutenant in the army.

Hap was a soldier during World War II. He was in the Third Armored Division Spearhead Tank Corps, under the leadership of General George S. Patton. That story has been told before in this column, but it bears repeating: Hap was a hero. He landed a tank on the beaches of Normandy. He fought through the Falaise Pocket. He took on Panzers (German armored vehicles) in the Battle of the Bulge. In the Hasternrath-Sherpanseel engagement in Germany, he earned a presidential unit citation. He fought in the Blitzkrieg campaign. He liberated a concentration camp near Nordhausen, and at nearby Sangerhaussen, he was the one who shot the lock off the gate.

He lost almost all his hearing in those tanks. He lost many of his friends in that war.

But Hap came back and married Nurse Vivian. He used to say that fighting Hitler was easier than raising three Paulson boys. He didn't talk much about the war, but he talked a lot about my Algebra homework.

He passed away six years ago. I wish that I could play one more game of cribbage. Or hug him one last time. What I can do is tell his story once a year and thank him for his service. To his country and to his family.

Wednesday is Veteran's Day. It started 101 years ago, originally known as Armistice Day, to recognize the sacrifice of servicemen who fought the "war to end all wars." But we still have wars, and we still have men and women who do brave things every day because they believe in honor and truth. So today, be kind to an older person who seems a little confused or doesn't hear that well. He or she may once have been a hero.

At some point, the D will fall off the Dad. But as the male parent becomes just another guy, remember: Like my father, he has a story.

iMac 'n Cheese

THE DOG ate Aidan's homework.

Aidan has spent more time fabricating excuses than he ever has actually doing homework. There was the time that he claimed he had amnesia. The time that he told Sister Lillian that I had taken his homework to my job to show all the other deputies how smart he was. The science experiment that rendered his notes invisible. But this time Aidan was telling the truth.

Thursday, Aidan and I spent an hour arguing about the Distributive Property, and another hour conjugating *hablar*. And in the age of Covid all of this is sent through the ether. I sat down at my old chestnut desk, clicked on a key. Nothing. Clicked the mouse. Dead air.

Aidan thought I crashed it because I didn't clean the keyboard, and I thought Aidan had crashed the desktop in a quest to rule the world of Minecraft.

One of our therapists told us to try not to assign blame, an important lesson in parenting teens, because I always guess wrong as to who poured dishwashing soap into the laundry, or who ate all the maple Oreo cookies. But after three hours of Algebra, someone had to take the fall.

I control-alt-deleted 'til I was blue in the face and still nothing. You can only turn off and on so many times, so I drove to the Apple Store in Stonestown.

Got home to the Outer, Outer, Outer, Outer Excelsior, with my spiffy new iMac, only to learn as I plugged it in (and unplugged the old one) it was Queenie who crashed the computer.

Readers may imagine that this came from her typing, but no, Queenie had eschewed chew toys and rawhide and greenies, deciding instead that nothing was more satisfying than Daddy's computer cables: iMac 'n cheese.

The screen showed me a picture of an island. Turns out that it's Santa Catalina, as in off the coast of Los Angeles, home to about 4100 people and a herd of bison.

Nothing against Southern California, but Brian's part wizard so he hates islands and crossing over water. Aidan shrugged, "Change the background" and showed me that iMac could search through our pictures, randomly put one up, and cascade through at a rate of one every half hour.

Did I know that my husband and I had 7,859 pictures? This means that we don't come up for a repeat for 327 days.

Pictures for us only became electronic about sixteen or seventeen years ago, and before that there's an entire shelf of albums from Polaroids and disposable cameras. But these seventeen years have been a lifetime, at least for my sons Zane and Aidan.

Up pops a shot from the trip to Disneyland, the four of us with Buzz Lightyear. Zane's first holy communion. The quilt that we made for Aidan's adoption. Christmas cards where we are dressed as the Avengers or the Village People. The Groundhog Day photo. This was the year Zane lived in Texas and we had missed Christmas together, and so Zane said, "Let's send out Groundhog Day cards!" Believe it or not, the guy who ran the only hotel in Fort Davis had never seen a family dressed up as woodchucks.

The difference between the Fisher-Paulsons of today and seventeen years ago is that with the electronic age, we can take twenty pictures, delete nineteen and save one. So out go the ones where Zane's smirking or I look fat; Aidan's not looking at the camera or I look fat; or Brian got exasperated that the three of us don't smile at the same time or I look fat.

As each picture rolls out onto the computer, I'm amazed that in almost all of them, we look happy. With all the expulsions, Covid-19 and fires, that somehow got neglected.

Here's the real homework: I need to remember that, even on the days your son has lost his homework again, all those moments together add up to at least 327 days of happy.

Quattordici

I T'S ALWAYS an adventure for our family, but why this adventure? After years of holiday disasters, I've learned to stop asking, "How could this get any worse?" One Thanksgiving Hap took us out to the movies so Nurse Vivian could finish the pies, only for all three sons to walk out of the theater with the measles. Then the one when Tim poured a cup of sugar into the mashed potatoes.

One year Brooklyn Union Gas turned off my power right after we put the turkey in the oven.

This year, shortly after I'd turned in last week's Thanksgiving column in fact, my husband Brian called: "Zane's school just let him know. His roommate tested positive. He gets tested in the morning. They want to know if we want him there or at home." Like that was really a question.

Shortly after, Zane texted, "I'm scared."

Nine months of washing hands, wearing a mask, maintaining six feet and then this happens. I texted back: "You're coming home now."

We've been following this pandemic forever. Zane's return meant that the Fisher-Paulsons would quarantine.

"Quarantine" comes from the Italian words *quaranta giorni*, which means 40 days. The term traces back to the amount of time ships that sailed into Venice needed to remain isolated during the Great Plague. It was originally 30 days, "*a trentine*," but they added a few after they reckoned that the average infection to death rate of the disease was 37 days. Even then there was an attempt to prove science works.

Since 14 days is in vogue for Covid-19, we should probably be calling it *quattordici*.

But quarantines just aren't what they used to be. I bet those guys in the leper colonies would love to have gotten touchless delivery from Mollie Stone's.

The Outer, Outer, Outer, Outer Excelsior never felt so outer than when the Bedlam Blue Bungalow started flying the yellow and black flag of quarantine. Four humans and three dogs settled in and waited. No Safeway. No Sheriff's Department. No Starbucks.

Brian watched Hallmark while I puttered. I'd never been away from work this long. The spices are now arranged in alphabetical order. The Rice-a-roni is sorted by flavor. Brian couldn't find Queenie the other night, so he looked in the file cabinet under "Q."

Scaling down Thanksgiving was a challenge. You can only get a turkey so small. The green bean casserole got canceled, as did yams. We were marooned on the Isle of Lost Pies.

Zane tested positive the Monday before, and the rest of us tested that day. Thanksgiving eve we got the news that we three were negative, but we test again next week.

Some of you may already be worried about Zane. He's been sleeping more, coughing a little bit, but is otherwise fine. Aidan, on the other side, has been waiting for this to happen. He's such a hypochondriac that literally if you ask the Merriam Webster online dictionary the meaning of "grippe" you will see Aidan's name.

When the teachers at Riordan posted online homework, Aidan was too feverish to read his assignments. When garbage day came, he was too weak to lift the pail. In fact, the only known cure for his malaise is the iPad, or an episode of *Teen Titans Go!*

One of you may remind me that Covid is nothing to joke about. This is not the Black Plague. This is not the Spanish Flu. But this is serious. Millions have been infected. Hundreds of thousands have died. And now the coronavirus has come to the Bedlam Blue Bungalow.

But this is how we face every crisis. We isolate. We take precautions. And we smile. We're all home, and we're together, and together we can face anything.

In the meantime, it wouldn't hurt for you to light a candle. We are all of us isolated, but none of us are alone.

See you physically in fourteen days.

Oh Quarantine!

YEARS FROM NOW, when we look back on it, our family will be grateful for this quarantine. Not for the epidemic, but for this fortnight.

This is the sequel to last week's column: Two weeks after we learned Zane's school roommate tested positive for Covid-19. I worried this was one more tragedy in a year of endless bad news. We moved Zane back in, and began our quarantine in the Outer, Outer, Outer, Outer Excelsior.

Thought this would be a long exile, but instead we learned to enjoy just being together. And we beat Aunt Rita.

Turns out that Zane had one of the mildest cases of coronavirus that anyone on this planet has had. He slept most of the time and had a continuous mild headache. If you've been reading the news, you know how lucky he is... must have been all the candles you readers lit.

Our family had never spent fourteen days just spending time together. I work a full-time job, and Brian typically juggles about five part-time jobs. During the average December, he's been known to perform in as many as two different Nutcrackers and a Velveteen Rabbit.

But we were on lockdown, where we couldn't go out, and the highlight of our day was the delivery from Mollie Stone's. We got to stop rushing around. We got to sit. And we got to listen.

When I think about it, this was a lot more fun than going to work.

We also must thank our neighbors. It's not until times like this that we remember to be grateful for this community, for the Terry Asten Bennett who dropped off milk and potatoes. When Deirdre had pâté and brie delivered, I said, "This is a lot better than walking around with a twenty-pound duty belt on."

Susan (the Roof Cow's Mom) baked for us, because even if we can't break bread, we can certainly take bread.

My father's sister, Aunt Rita, turned 97 this year, the last of her generation. There's a rite of passage in the Paulson family: When you get your own separate Christmas card from Aunt Rita, you know that you are an adult. I had lived for 27 years on the planet before I was no longer part of "Hap and Viv… and Family." But "Kevin Paulson… somewhere in Hoboken."

And hers was always the first card to arrive. She must have started the day after Halloween, but always on Black Friday, every one of us could count on a high-class envelope with silver foil lining coming from Hicksville by way of the North Pole.

Not like the Fisher-Paulsons. We've done 35 Christmas cards, and all of them with high production values but little class. The last twenty, we've done after Thanksgiving with Crazy Mike driving us to Sutro Tower or the Cliff House, to photograph four humans and various hounds dressed as pirates (AAARgh! The Herald Angels Sing!) or the Village People (Your Merry Christmas Angels).

But quarantine changed that tradition. We couldn't even let Crazy Mike into the Bedlam Blue Bungalow. And so this year, just the four of us, with festive sweaters on, took a picture and sent it off to production a week before Thanksgiving.

On a lazy Wednesday afternoon, we sat and addressed a few hundred envelopes. Brian, who is not competitive, said, "Hurry up and put them in the mailbox."

It took 62 years, but our cards finally arrived before Aunt Rita's.

Nothing makes me feel more Christmasy than beating my non-agenarian aunt.

Somewhere in the world, there is a Paulson nephew saying, "Next year, we'll beat Uncle Kevin!"

I got my second negative test results on December 3rd and was cleared to return to the Sheriff's Department.

I'm happy about the badge and all, but a part of me will miss these cozy mornings, when the dawn comes late and lazy. When Zane asks for hot chocolate and Aidan for waffles, and we get out the Avengers waffle iron and sit at the table with a fresh batch of Hulks and Captain Americas, our mugs spilling whipped cream as we toast.

Queenie sits under the table, wagging her tail, because she knows: We are together, and without this quarantine, we might not have known how blessed we are.

Tom and Jerry

B RIAN AND I moved to San Francisco in 1991 and found an apartment in the Mission, on Fair Oak Street. Before we unpacked, I leashed the dogs for a walk. They hadn't circumnavigated their first California block before they sniffed a poodle, who turned out to be Armistead Maupin's companion.

Back east, we were enchanted by *Tales of the City* and the mysterious coincidences that happened here. For him to be our first coincidence was a sign. This was in August, and as fictional San Francisco became real as we embraced the hills and the fog. It did bother me that it never rained, and as the weather turned cold, it was unlikely to ever snow on these 49 square miles.

I missed Christmas in New York that December. I was nostalgic, not for the slush I walked through or the smell of burnt chestnuts but rather, for Radio City with Nurse Vivian (and the Rockettes).

But one night, as I teetered on the verge of homesickness and rounded the turn on 21st Street with the dogs, we saw lights near the top of the hill.

We crossed Church and climbed to find a Norfolk pine, more than 60 feet high, taller than the one in Rockefeller Center and decorated in a style that can be described as "only in San Francisco": Giant stockings, a miniature roller coaster, a rainbow flag, with a neighborhood of stars behind it. And Santa was there, handing out candy canes to the children.

That day San Francisco became my hometown, because here

people grew their own magic. And then put tinsel on it. From Armistead, and Herb Caen, I knew not to call it Frisco, so I started calling it Frank.

It wouldn't be for a few years, when I met the Terry Asten Bennett, that I got the story behind the Miracle on 21st Street. Tom Taylor and Jerry Goldstein (a.k.a. Tom and Jerry) took in a houseplant somewhere around 1970. When it outgrew the pot, around 1973, Tom planted it to the yard. That December, he put on ornaments and lights and that led to Ferris wheels and life-size dolls.

They did this just to be kind to the neighbors. And Tom and Jerry did other nice things: they took care of the Rainbow flag at Castro and Market. They founded the Diversity Foundation of San Francisco.

But their tree was part of our Christmas. Every year after midnight mass at Most Holy Redeemer Church, we took Zane and Aidan there on the way home. Aidan always said he could hear sleigh bells overhead.

For the past few weeks, this column has chronicled the Fisher-Paulson quarantine in the Outer, Outer, Outer, Outer Excelsior, which means a virtual holiday. Mark Foehringer's *Nutcracker Sweets* went online, as did ODC's *Velveteen Rabbit*.

What would endure?

Tom Taylor died in October. We didn't know if Jerry would continue the tradition. I'd like to think that if Brian goes before me that I'll still set up the Christmas village, but the truth is I don't even know how to plug it in.

And so, last week with a little trepidation, I walked up 21st Street.

As I neared the summit, I thought that the hill has gotten steeper in the past 29 years.

Then I saw a team of about four nice guys screwing in light bulbs.

One of the workers, Hunter, told me that it takes four or five weeks. But it's worth it. For the rest of the month, the tree gets more downhill traffic than Lombard Street.

If you drive by, wave, but do not honk. And if you're feeling adventurous, walk up from the Mission.

That's what Frank is about. The little coincidences. The little kindnesses. And the big ones.

Headless Saint

T HE HEADLESS SAINT. This is where gratitude starts.

In South Ozone Park, Nurse Vivian didn't decorate for Thanksgiving. She skipped straight into Christmas: snowmen made of dry-cleaning bags, stockings sewed in felts and sequins.

She had purchased a manger scene in the Woolworth's in Johnstown, PA. She set it up on top of the Zenith color television, so that on commercials and at half time, the family could contemplate the Christmas miracle.

One year the shepherd went missing. We never solved that mystery, though I've always suspected Brother X.

It never bothered Nurse Vivian, who used to say, "The shepherd was a bit player. Things go missing. That's how family works."

I'm not unlike Nurse Vivian. We don't have Thanksgiving decorations, so November gets dedicated to Brian setting up his Christmas Village (technically, with 130 buildings, it's a Christmas megalopolis) while I set up sheep and oxen.

We've got more Nativities than any other family in the Outer, Outer, Outer, Outer Excelsior: one's made of straw, carved in wood. Another made of pewter. In fact, we're running out of room at the inn. We got one outside: a blomold that lights up, the pageant of the electric virgin. John, foster father to the roof cow, has suggested that our outdoor manger should feature two Josephs, no Mary and a disco ball for the Star of Bethlehem, but we're trying not to get kicked out of the neighborhood.

But the *crèche de la resistance* is in the dining room china cabinet. Brian's not a Woolworth kind of husband, so we set up a Swarovski Nativity: Austrian crystal depicting the lowly manger.

This year, there won't be holiday gatherings. Brian and I wondered whether it was worth it to drag the cartons out of the basement and decorate a bungalow that only the Fisher-Paulsons would see. But in the end, we reasoned, the boys seeing it was enough.

In fact, Zane and Aidan carried up the boxes. I unpacked and arranged angels and sheep. Mary stage right, Joseph stage left, with the Magi hovering near the proscenium. But Melchior wouldn't stand up straight, so as I stood him up yet again, I clipped Joseph with my sweatshirt.

He tumbled to the floor and lost his head, looking a lot more like John the Baptist after his date with Salome than he did a carpenter on vacation in Bethlehem.

I cursed myself out (*en francais*) because even though Nurse Vivian could live with the loss of a shepherd, clearly Joseph was central to the whole Bethlehem stable.

You'd think that in the Bedlam Blue Bungalow we'd have an extra foster father lying around, but there's never a good saint when you need one. Brian looked me right in the eye and added, "And we're even shorter on wise men."

The bright side? It was clumsiness, not malice, that decapitated the foster father of God. Not Queenie teething. Not Zane's tantrum. The statue lost his head. But none of us did. And that is our Thanksgiving miracle.

It's a smaller group around the table this year. We love to host Uncle Jon, Aunt Dee and Uncle Howard, Jill and Sarah, Deirdre, but the responsible thing is to make a smaller turkey and bake a few less pies.

It's what we do in a tough year: the age of the Covid-19 pandemic, the isolation, social unrest, homelessness and Lightning Strike fires.

But when we sit down to table, hold hands and say Grace, that's not what we're thinking about. This year's lesson: find the blessing in being together.

It's as simple as this: avoid being ungrateful for what you don't have. Be grateful for what you do have, no matter how small. Even when we are eclipsed, standing in the darkness, we see that at the edge there is light.

Afterword

Y EARS AGO, Jill Tucker set me up for lunch with David Wiegand, editor of the Datebook section of the San Francisco Chronicle. We had lamb chops and bourbon at John's Grill, and during the meal David told me that he was looking for five columnists to replace the great Jon Carroll, one for each day of the work week.

Jill had shown him an email that I had written to her and a few other friends, about Zane's first armpit hair. David said that I expressed a slice of the uniqueness of San Francisco: a gay deputy sheriff and his modern dance husband (the deputy and the dance hall girl) raising a black son and a mixed-race son and harboring rescue dogs — all living in a Bedlam Blue Bungalow on the very edge of San Francisco. He told me that our story would follow the long tradition of San Francisco newspaper writers: Mark Twain, Jack London, Brett Harte, Art Hoppe, Adair Lara, Armistead Maupin, Leah Garchik, and, of course, Herb Caen. We walked back to the Chronicle office after lunch, and there, under glass, was the Loyal Royal upon which Caen's columns had been typed.

I am a lucky man. I have typed in the shadow of giants. For eight years now I have appeared on the very last page of the newspaper, above the fold, and as each week has gone by, as I have typed I have learned more about myself.

We are in the internet age when newspapers are struggling to keep their audience, but there are readers, thousands of them, who still like to see the news dropped on their doorstep, with gossip about the mayor, the comics, and the results of the Giants game all in one place.

I am a lucky man. Every Wednesday for years, I have had coffee with the greater San Francisco Bay area, and I'm on a first name basis with all of them. The Outer, Outer, Outer, Outer Excelsior stretches from Geneva Avenue to Rome to Uruguay and New Zealand.

This column made me a better writer. This column taught me that in an ever-changing world, there are some things which must always be constant, like kindness and family.

I am a lucky man. Almost forty years ago, I stumbled into a relationship with Brian, a man with whom I would move across the country and come to live in the best city in the world, a city that is also on a first name basis with me: Frank. We chose family and we keep choosing family and, against all odds, we have fostered, adopted and raised two sons, Zane and Aidan.

This book is a collection of columns from 2019 and 2020. The pandemic and the fires and that crazy election are all behind us. The world is very different now. Zane has graduated high school and is going through the longest gap year in history. Aidan is now a senior at Compass High School, loved by his teachers because he is such a compassionate and quirky young man.

Buddyboy and Bandit have crossed to the other side, and our dog Queenie adopted her own rescue dog, Moxie. The Kipcap's been in three accidents, and yet still rolls.

Brian went through a health crisis. He lost a toe, which ended his career as a dancer. At this writing I am going through my own crisis with cancer, and I might not work much longer as a deputy sheriff. But I still write for the Chronicle, and I will keep writing every Wednesday for as long as the Voice of the West will have me. Only while going through my challenge did I find out how loyal and loving the readers of the San Francisco Chronicle are. They have chosen me as their columnist, and I am humbled by their support.

The Bedlam Bungalow is still blue. We are still surrounded by ceanothus trees, and fat honeybees still hover around the edges. Karlotta the Fog still visits Frank in the summer.

The Fisher-Paulsons are still a mismatched family, prone to breaking things. But in all these years, we've discovered that we are not unique. We have chosen each other as family and we keep choosing each other day after day, year after year, despite the detentions, the dining room burning down, the magnets in the sewage line, the head stuck in the staircase.

Zane and Aidan are now adults. They make their own choices. Parents never really know what they have passed on to their children, but so far both of these young men seem to have adopted the Fisher-Paulson Family Motto: **When in doubt, be kind.**

I am a lucky man.

Thank you for reading.

Also by Kevin Fisher-Paulson

the heart-rending true story of an American family

What makes a family? And what are the real "family values" that help keep parents and children whole and healthy? In *A Song for Lost Angels*, Kevin Fisher-Paulson answers these questions by telling the intimate history of a family of two men plus triplets that came together suddenly one day, and thrived for a year before being torn apart by groundless prejudice. And he tells this riveting story with grace, dignity, and a surprisingly generous dose of humor.

This title was a triple finalist in two independent publishing competitions, the Benjamin Franklin Awards and Next Generation Indie Book Awards. Originally published by Fearless Books, the 2nd Edition was released under the author's own imprint, Two Penny Press. Order through your local bookstore or online at *www.fearlessbooks.com/Song.htm*.

the journey of a family in stories

At any given moment, the journey of a family is the sum of its stories. Kevin Fisher-Paulson is beloved throughout the San Francisco Bay area and beyond for the stories of family he has told as a weekly columnist for the *San Francisco Chronicle*. While telling his stories, Kevin has stumbled over more than a few truths about foster care, gay marriage, interracial family, rescue dogs, and cupcakes.

The stories of a deputy and a dancer along the journey of raising two challenging boys in the Outer, Outer, Outer, Outer Excelsior have drawn a loyal readership of interracial and adoptive families, families dealing with learning challenges and disabilities, gays and lesbians, and people who love San Francisco. This first collection of Kevin's columns can be ordered through your local bookstore or online at *www.fearlessbooks.com/Spinning.htm*.

All three of Kevin's books have been produced in association with Fearless Books & Literary Services, an independent publisher and editorial agency founded by D. Patrick Miller. For more information see *www.fearlessbooks.com*.

Printed in the USA
CPSIA information can be obtained
at www.ICGtesting.com
LVHW040852151123
763329LV00002B/6/J